AMERICAN STRATEGY:
A NEW PERSPECTIVE

AMERICAN STRATEGY:
A NEW PERSPECTIVE

The Growth of Politico-Military
Thinking in the United States

URS SCHWARZ

PREFACE BY HENRY A. KISSINGER

Doubleday & Company, Inc.
Garden City, New York
1966

LIBRARY OF CONGRESS CATALOG CARD NUMBER 66–15443

COPYRIGHT © 1965 BY ECON VERLAG GMBH,
DÜSSELDORF AND VIENNA
COPYRIGHT © 1966 BY ECON VERLAG GMBH
PREFACE COPYRIGHT © 1966 BY DOUBLEDAY & COMPANY, INC.

Contents

Author's Note

The wish to write a comprehensive study on the growth of strategic thinking in the United States of America developed out of my editorial writing in the *Neue Zürcher Zeitung,* my reviewing of strategic literature in the post-war period, and my speaking to military and civilian groups on problems of and views on strategy in the atomic age. Time and again I was struck, in the course of discussions, by the amount of incomprehension concerning the work of American strategic thinkers, and the hostility expressed, even by well-meaning people, to a rational discussion of politico-military problems confronting the world. I felt that reasons for this attitude in Europe were similar to reasons that in America, for more than a century, had prevented a serious discussion of national strategy. In spite of the arms debate which developed in the United States in the late forties, I discovered that even the interested observer, civic leader and scientist in America found it difficult to follow the development of strategic thought. I came to think that a book surveying the whole field and tracing the development back to its roots might be needed. I felt that a European observer might find it easier to write such a book than any of the American authors who are so involved in the subject, who belong so much to definite schools of thought, to the armed services, to government departments, to institutes.

The book will not deal specifically with the criticism of and resistance to strategic science and analysis, but rather with existing strategic thought, its origins and its future development. Criticisms of strategic theory as such, which stem from as diverse sources as the military profession and the liberal intellectuals, might well be the object of a separate study. They are directed against certain theories, patterns of thinking and modes of expression, and their application to politico-military planning, or against the use of military power as a means of foreign policy. As this study will show, and as recent events have proved, the effect of these voices on the actual development of politico-military affairs has been very limited.

I was encouraged to undertake the task by Professor Thomas C. Schelling of the Harvard University Center for International Affairs, with whom I had discussed my plan at conferences of the Institute for Strategic Studies, the International Committee of the Red Cross, and the Center for International Affairs itself. The decisive encouragement came from the Harvard Center which made it possible for me to leave the editorial offices in Zurich for a period of time that I could devote fully to writing this study. I am indebted to the Director of the Center for International Affairs, Professor Robert Bowie, for his constructive advice, to Professor Henry A. Kissinger for his encouragement, and especially to Professor Schelling, who introduced me to a great number of writers and scholars, government agencies, both military and civilian, and many private institutions.

Wherever I went, I was aided in gathering first-hand information about strategic thinking, past, present and future. Among the institutions that helped me, I wish to mention especially the Washington Center of Foreign Policy Research and its Director, Arnold Wolfers, the Hudson Institute and its Director, Herman Kahn, the United States Military Academy's Department of Social Sciences, Colonel George A. Lincoln, and The RAND Corporation, particularly Bernard Brodie, Robert A. Levine, Richard Latter, Herbert S. Dinerstein, and Brownlee Haydon. Many of these people read a first draft of my manuscript and offered constructive criticism.

I am indebted to a number of fellows and research associates of the Center for International Affairs and to Mrs. Elizabeth Miller (Cambridge, Mass.), the widow of my late friend Professor Perry Miller, who revised the first draft of my English manuscript.

Finally I owe a testimony of gratitude to the *Neue Zürcher Zeitung* and the *Swiss Review of World Affairs*, which throughout the years gave me all the space I ever wanted for articles about strategic problems, and which granted me the leave of absence necessary to write this study.

Zurich, Switzerland,
Spring, 1966

Preface

What Americans think about their power determines the security of their friends and sets the framework for the calculations of their opponents. While American power is no guarantee for a constructive foreign policy, no constructive foreign policy is possible without it.

It has always been true that until power is used, it is what people think it is. Throughout history, strategic doctrine has determined which of the available choices in weapons, tactics or policy a state would, in fact, follow. Doctrine as used here should not be considered as something abstract and esoteric: Rather it defines the likely challenges and how to deal with them; it specifies the possible goals and how to attain them. Its test is whether what it defines as probable is in fact the most frequent occurrence and whether its prescribed mode of action turns out to be relevant to the problems at hand.

This historic role of strategic doctrine has been magnified in the nuclear age. Weapons are novel and untested. A technology of unprecedented destructiveness is allied with a rate of change which produces obsolescence every five years. Many of our critics in Western Europe cite the changes American strategic doctrine has undergone in the last two decades as proof of the fickleness of American policy. However, given the rate of technological change they should be more

concerned were the United States to cling to obsoles-
cent conceptions rather than when it seeks to adapt
its doctrine to new realities.

Because of the enormous destructiveness of modern
weapons, their most important function is deterrence:
to prevent an undesirable action by a threat. But the
deterrent relationship is largely psychological. Its effectiveness depends on the calculations of the side
being threatened, not of the side which makes the
threat. For purposes of deterrence a threat which is
meant as a bluff but is taken seriously is more useful
than a serious threat which is interpreted as a bluff.
Psychology, policy, technology and strategy therefore
merge.

Moreover, deterrence is tested negatively by actions
or events which do *not* take place. It is impossible,
however, to demonstrate why something has *not* occurred. It can never be proved whether peace has
been maintained because the existing strategic doctrine is the best possible or whether it is only margin-
ally effective. Indeed it cannot even be demonstrated
conclusively whether there was any danger of attack
in the first place. Thus side by side with the elabora-
tion of strategic doctrine there has developed a school
of thought challenging its value and necessity.

Despite the central importance of strategic doctrine,
it has emerged only recently as a theoretical discipline
in the United States. To be sure, the United States has
developed strategic plans ever since the early days of
the Republic. And writers in military affairs have had
a major influence shaping particular military services
—such as Mahan with respect to the navy. But strategic doctrine as the interplay of political and military
factors has been inhibited by an American tradition
which viewed war and peace as discrete phases of

policy. In this concept, war was conducted on the basis of purely military considerations; to intrude "politics" into it was considered wrong, even immoral. Until victory was achieved the diplomats had to stand aside. Unconditional surrender has therefore been a traditional American war aim.

By the same token during periods of peace, American policy-makers have often acted as if international relations were like a gigantic debate in which victory went to the side presenting the most reasonable arguments. The relationship of power and foreign policy was insufficiently recognized. This separation of power and policy had the result that military policy frequently took the form of simply amassing resources; while diplomacy tended to confuse legal formulae with substantive achievement.

Only the last decade and a half has seen an attempt to merge these two realms. But precisely because the field of strategic doctrine in its widest sense was so new, those engaged in developing a theory for it sometimes forget the wood for the trees. Conscious of disagreements over more or less esoteric fine points, they have occasionally refined sophisticated elaborations at the expense of an over-all approach.

It is the great merit of Urs Schwarz's splendid little book, that it brings together all of the relevant thinking about American strategic doctrine. He traces the history of American strategic thought, showing the traditional sharp division between military affairs and foreign policy and its gradual erosion after World War II. He devotes over two-thirds of his book to significant trends in American strategic thought since the end of World War II. With extraordinary skill, he presents the various strands of American strategic thinking, both governmental and academic.

His success in this effort is no accident. As foreign editor of the most distinguished newspaper in the German language—the *Neue Zürcher Zeitung*—Mr. Schwarz combines an acute power of observation with the ability to write tersely and precisely. As a Swiss, he is in the fortunate position of being able to maintain sufficient detachment to distinguish the essential from the peripheral. I know of no American who could have presented the American strategic debate so fairly. Those of us who have admired Mr. Schwarz's writings in the past can only be grateful that his thought on a subject of such vital importance for all free peoples is now available to an American audience.

Henry A. Kissinger

I

Thought and Experience
in World War I

The American's thinking is deeply rooted in his view of history. His beliefs and the decisions based thereon are shaped to an extraordinary degree by historic precedent, by what has happened to his country or what his schools have made him believe has happened. He is equaled, perhaps, only by the Chinese in his deep pragmatic involvement with his own past, of which he is proud, and which gives him guidance in today's decisions.

The American historian Edwin O. Reischauer writes

. . . the Chinese have always been historically minded, prone to take the historical approach to any subject or situation. The writing of history was always an important function of government in China, and as a result the Chinese were inveterate and extremely good historians.[1]

We might substitute the word "Americans" for "Chinese" to describe quite accurately the situation prevailing in the United States.

A glance at the 140-page index of the *Harvard Guide to American History* gives us a quick but strong

[1] *Japan, Past and Present* (New York, 1953), p. 29.

1

impression of the deep involvement of America and the Americans in their own past.[2]

Since this past, owing to centuries of insularity—real or imaginary—consists less of political events than of political thought, traditional political thinking has knit a tight web around the American mind. The military mind everywhere is naturally inclined to rely on tradition rather than on speculation. This held true for American military thinking until the shattering experience of World War II. When, in earlier periods, thought thus shaped and influenced was confronted with the realities of war, it either shaped events so that they might adjust to thought, or it experienced a revolutionary change. The first took place when all the events remained within America's reach, as they did in the Civil War and in the Spanish-American War. The second occurred, however, when the United States was confronted with international reality; this happened in the two World Wars.

When the first great war in Europe entered upon its depressing, bloody first winter, President Woodrow Wilson, in his annual message to Congress on December 8, 1914, could not help referring to the concern existing in the country over the disproportion between its size, its importance in world affairs and its military power. He expressed in forceful words what American strategy must mean. The first definition was a negative one: America must never have a standing army. To be prepared did not mean being able to put an army into the field at short notice, and America would never conceivably, in time of peace, be ready to do that so long as it retained its political principles and institutions. America, he affirmed, would always

[2] Cambridge, Mass., 1963.

2

be ready to defend itself to the utmost, "yet we shall not turn America into a military camp." Rather, the nation should depend on citizens trained and accustomed to arms. And in order to make such a passive strategy of defense more plausible, the President interpreted the war then going on as "a war with which we have nothing to do, whose causes cannot touch us."

WILSON AND THE NAVY

The realities of American defense were far from corresponding to Wilson's—and many others'—image of an armed citizenry. The President was deeply disturbed by the sight of a powerful navy, of which he was the commander-in-chief. It sounds pathetic to us to learn that, speaking in New York on May 17, 1915, to the officers of the Atlantic Fleet, he described naval vessels as merely defensive in character and the officers as simple citizens who, because of their close affinity with the whole American people, would inevitably know how to use their engines in the interest of humanity.[3] President Wilson exclaimed:

> These quiet ships lying in the river have no suggestion of bluster about them, no intimation of aggression. They are commanded by men thoughtful of the duty of citizens as well as the duty of officers . . . men who know by touch with the people of the United States . . . what sort of discretion they ought to exercise in order to use those engines of force as engines to promote the interests of humanity.

Contrary to what Wilson sought to assert the U. S. Navy, which by its very nature called for professional skill and professional personnel, had left far behind

[3] Edgar E. Robinson and Victor J. West, *The Foreign Policy of Woodrow Wilson, 1913–1917* (New York, 1918), p. 266.

the concept of the armed citizenry so dear to most American politicians, historians and leaders. The Navy was considered, from the outset, by the more realistic advocates of an adequate national defense, as the permanent element for the protection and defense of the "vast national interests and honor," while the small standing army, as the "model and instructor," would permit the United States to rely on the mobilization of its patriotic citizens in case of an emergency. This disposition would, as Lieutenant General John M. Schofield wrote in 1897, correspond to the "perfect ideal of a peace-loving yet military republic."[4]

From July 3, 1775, when George Washington assumed command of the forces that were to achieve the independence of the United Colonies, until November 3, 1783, when he disbanded his army, he had been beset with the problems of an utterly insufficient military establishment. He had to fight the distrust of the Congress and the people, who deeply believed in the axiom that "standing armies are dangerous to liberty." He had constantly to fight the deficiencies of a military system under which volunteers and militia were mobilized by the legislatures for a limited period only and then disbanded, and he had to fight a complete and persistent lack of discipline, which found expression in frequent mutinies, as well as the effects of a deplorable system of logistics.

In his defense of the Federal Constitution Alexander Hamilton was forced to go to great lengths to explain why there should be no clause copied from the Declaration of Rights of 1774 to the effect that "Standing armies are dangerous to Liberty."[5] Educated Americans might be familiar with the history of the British

[4] *Forty-six Years in the Army* (New York, 1897), p. 366.
[5] *The Federalist,* no. 24.

Civil War of the preceding century, and live with the heroes of Greek and Roman history and their example of civic virtue. But, far more vivid and present to the consciousness of the common people were stories of the wars against France, when American militiamen had fought in the service of the Crown of England, often ill treated by British officers, while the regular British troops behaved as professional soldiers would behave in a wild and less than friendly country.

These deeply rooted sentiments, which were an integral part of American thinking and American folklore, and which were at the very center of the wish for American independence, prevented any serious rethinking or reform. In spite of certain timid measures adopted by Congress, the same mistakes were made in the War of 1812. That its political issue was more favorable than its military result, which was at best a draw and came close to a British victory, was due to the situation prevailing in Europe. The British agreed to re-establish the *status quo ante* because of the threat of Napoleon, which prevented them from engaging much larger forces in America.

American political and historical literature is full of the accounts of military unpreparedness throughout the nineteenth century. The Civil War bore testimony time and again to the specific American thinking on war and national defense, its rejection of a professional army, its belief in ad hoc forces and amateurs of every kind.

Upon the conclusion of the Civil War, one of the outstanding generals of the war, Major General Emory Upton, was sent around the world with two associate officers to study the armies of Asia and Europe. His report, which embodied the practical lessons of the Civil War and his observations throughout the world,

5

was not even printed by the government. Upton's subsequent book, *The Military Policy of the United States,* nearly finished at the time of the author's death in 1881,[6] called strongly for the necessary reforms.

Another less professional but more original contribution to American strategic writing, published in the early years of the twentieth century, renewed the indictment of the traditional tendencies of *laisser-aller.* The book is Homer Lea's *The Valor of Ignorance,* which was published in 1909, highly praised by some military officers, read by few and soon forgotten.[7]

Lea, a passionate Far Eastern specialist, devoted his book to showing how, contrary to the common belief, the continental United States and the American possessions lay open to aggression and invasion. A chapter with an imaginary Japanese invasion of the Philippines—which thirty-three years later was to follow exactly the lines drawn by Lea—concludes with the following reflection:

> The defence of the Philippines belongs, not alone to an army or navy or fortified harbors, but to an intelligent combination of them all. This defence cannot be relegated to those expedients that are alone consequent upon sudden war, but must be inherent in the national policy of the Republic and the military preparations of prior years. It cannot be left to the shifts of unforeseen combat, but must be predetermined by existent conditions and such works as the knowledge and labor of man may evolve out of the Science of War.[8]

[6] Not published until 1904 (in Washington), when a great Secretary of War, Elihu Root, rescued it from oblivion.
[7] Republished with an introduction by Clare Boothe (New York, 1942).
[8] Ibid., pp. 254 f.

The works and letters of Theodore Roosevelt, throughout the last decade of the nineteenth and the first decade of the twentieth centuries, are full of admonitions to the American people that political aspirations have to be consonant with a military posture, by which he almost exclusively meant naval power. But his remained, as clearly expressed by the sometimes extreme bitterness of his remarks, a lonely voice.

AFTER POLITICS: WAR

The political evolution of the United States out of isolation into the First World War and its corollary in strategy are well known. On March 5, 1917, at his second inauguration, President Wilson could say: "We are provincials no longer. The tragical events of the thirty months of vital turmoil through which we have just passed have made us citizens of the world. There can be no turning back." And on April 2, 1917, the President asked Congress to authorize a declaration of war on Germany.

Now emerged the second element of American strategic thought. The instinct of isolation was spent, the concept of a merely civilian defense posture abandoned—completely superseded by the determination to destroy the enemy utterly. It came forward majestically in the President's words: "We . . . shall, if necessary, spend the whole force of the nation to check and nullify its [the enemy's] pretensions and its power. . . . We are glad . . . to fight thus for the ultimate peace of the world and for the liberation of its peoples. . . . The world must be made safe for democracy."[9]

This extremely generalized pronouncement on strat-

[9] Robinson and West, op. cit., p. 382.

7

egy and war aims introduced the tremendous war effort that America was to perform in the coming nineteen months.

The small existing army was scattered in regiments over the entire nation. There were no divisions, no army corps, and no corresponding staffs. There were no strategic plans. There was no machinery for cooperation with Britain and France. Hence the creation of a force able to defeat Germany became necessarily the first and only concern.

As early as March 31, 1917, Admiral William S. Sims had been dispatched, at the request of the British Government, to London. He arrived there after the American declaration of war had been served. His mission was to co-ordinate the war effort of the U. S. Navy with the British, and he carried it out brilliantly until the end of the war. In his exchanges of dispatches with Washington the prevailing views on strategy soon became apparent. America's first aim was "the termination of the present war." Wilson was highly critical of the British because they did not seem to use their naval superiority to that end. He was doubtful of the convoy system and unhappy about the anti-submarine war, and he declared that the Navy was like a man hunting hornets all over the farm and letting the nest alone. And again the President expressed his deep doubts about the military profession—which he shared with many of his countrymen—when he wrote that this war, being completely unprecedented, was therefore, in a sense, a war for amateurs.[10]

Americans always liked to contrast their strategic concepts with those of Britain; it happened in the First World War, was an important theme of discord

[10] Elting E. Morison, *Admiral Sims and the Modern American Navy* (Boston, 1942), pp. 359–61.

among Allies in the Second World War, and played a role again in the Korean War. When, in the Senate hearings on the Military Situation in the Far East in 1951 (MacArthur Hearings), Senator Hickenlooper criticized the British for their uncertain attitude, he said: ". . . our military tactics and strategy in this country have always been of an aggressive nature; we believe in getting the thing over with; we believe in an aggressiveness rather than muddling through."[11]

PERSHING IN EUROPE

When, on May 26, 1917, General John J. Pershing was appointed commander-in-chief of the American Expeditionary Forces in Europe, he sailed, without delay, to Europe, accompanied by a small staff. It was only after conferences with the British staff in London and the French staff in Paris that ideas began to emerge as to what could and should be done by the American forces in this conjuncture. It was from Europe that Pershing proposed building up an army of one million men to be in France by May, 1918, with the further intention of training an additional two million men in anticipation of possible later need. One division was to be organized at once from existing regiments and sent to France. Elements of this advance force paraded on July 4, 1917, down the Champs Elysées, to the great relief of the population of Paris.

It was from Europe that General Pershing sent his plans for the organization of the future army, for the composition of future divisions, their staffs and combat units. It was in Europe that within a few weeks

[11] *Military Situation in the Far East.* Hearings before the Committee on Armed Services and the Committee on Foreign Relations, U. S. Senate, 82d Congress, 1st session (Washington, 1951), p. 493.

Pershing and his small staff set up the program for the training of the new American army.

Thereupon, suddenly, a battered Europe was confronted with a strategic concept to which the Americans would cling unflinchingly throughout the coming months of the war, a concept challenged time and again by the Allied powers, but never relinquished by the American High Command. Whenever, momentarily, adjustments had to be made under the strain of immediate crises, it was always reverted to as quickly as possible. The extraordinary ease—almost casualness—with which a sketchily organized American staff could promulgate a strategic as well as a tactical doctrine can only be explained by the existence of a predetermined pattern of thought, common to all Americans and tacitly accepted as immutable truth.

Pershing's orders, endorsed by the President, were for the creation of an American expeditionary corps with its logistical base in the United States, and joined to it by the umbilical cord of American shipping and an American railroad system between the French ports and the front. This expeditionary corps was to remain an independent American army, operating as such, and was not to be put at the disposal of the Allied powers wherever the need might be most pressing.

On the Western front, trench warfare had been forced upon the armies for more than two years in spite of their desire to remain on the offensive. All attempts on the part of the Germans as well as of the Allied powers to regain freedom of maneuver had failed. When Pershing arrived in France, the French High Command and nation were still under the impact of the failure of the April offensive named after General Nivelle, which in spite of the offensive spirit and the gallantry of the troops had bogged down under artillery and machine-gun fire among trenches and barbed wire. Pershing at once announced that, so far as American troops were concerned, "the basis of instruction should be essentially the offensive both in spirit and in practice. The defensive is accepted only to prepare for future offensive."[12]

But an independent American army had to be trained. The assistance of the British and the French, who by now commanded enormous experience, was offered and readily accepted. American divisions, it was agreed, would train along with French divisions. American officers would attend the training centers of the Allies. Under the so-called Six-division Plan the British obtained the right, in exchange for providing transportation across the Atlantic, to use American battalions, under the pretext of training, as reinforcements for their own depleted divisions. These were minor accommodations. Still, Pershing insisted on the two essentials: as soon as feasible, American troops would form American divisions, the divisions would form American army corps, and the corps an American army, which would thus engage the enemy in a sector of its own. Both the strategic and tactical doctrine governing training and combat would be American. The aim was the resumption of a vigorous offensive. Accepted general principles would remain unchanged and all existing service manuals would continue to be the guides of officers and soldiers.

In the meantime, the colossal effort of mobilizing manpower in the United States and of harnessing the industrial potential for the war effort bore fruit. When, on March 21, 1918, the Germans launched the first of

[12] "Final Report of General John J. Pershing, September 1, 1919," *A History of Military Affairs*, Gordon B. Turner, ed. (New York, 1956), p. 386.

their 1918 offensives, conceived as decisive and designed to win the war, 300,000 American soldiers were in France. Four strong divisions, each equivalent to two French or British divisions, were ready to be engaged. On July 15, when the Germans started their last and abortive offensive, 1,200,000 American soldiers stood prepared. On September 12, 1918, an American army consisting of three corps, including a few French divisions, supported by French, British, and American air forces, opened the decisive offensive between the Moselle and the Meuse.

American participation was not limited, however, to the initial supply of stop-gap assistance and the later one of a powerful independent army. The influence of the freshly arrived combatants went much deeper. The Americans brought with them the offensive spirit, which they had inherited from a century of single-minded military instruction. The European armies had continued to adhere to the dogma of the superiority of the offensive over the defensive, in spite of their cruel experience with the defensive strength of modern fire power, but found it difficult to apply. The Americans renewed their confidence in the possibility of an offensive. They brought, in addition, their strong belief in the concentration of forces. When finally, on April 3, 1918, at Beauvais, the Supreme War Council appointed Marshal Foch as High Commander, it was done not only because of the immediate crisis, but also because of the strong views held by Pershing and General Tasker H. Bliss, the President's representative on the Supreme Council.

It is interesting to note, and not without significance, that Britain, France and Italy were generally represented in the Council by the highest government authority, whereas the United States spoke through mili-

tary men. General Bliss' opinions as to the necessity
of a unified command were well known. He had expressed them forcefully as early as December 1917
when he said, in a report to the President: "National
jealousies and suspicions and susceptibilities of national temperament must be put aside in favor of this
unified control; even going if necessary (as I believe
it is) to the limit of unified command."[13]

When, surprisingly, the war ended on November 11,
1918, the American war machine, by then in highest
gear, was grinding out new armies and new material.
A huge air force was in the making. American military
strategy—in terms of concentration and offensive—had
conquered. But what was to come?

WILSON AND WAR AIMS

In an address on May 27, 1916, long before America's entry into the contest, President Wilson had advocated that upon the conclusion of the war some as-
sociation of nations should be established which would
make future conflicts impossible. In his many war
speeches he had urged the nations to accept certain
principles of moral behavior, which he finally enunciated, in the so-called Fourteen Points, in his address
to Congress on January 8, 1918. It is noteworthy
that his war aims seemed at the outset extremely
vague, and merely the restatement of general principles of national and international law and morality
—just war, freedom of the seas, self-determination of
small nations, sovereignty of the people. Yet, while the
war effort of the nation grew, while news of death and
suffering reached the deeply religious man in the

[13] Ibid., p. 410.

13

White House, the war aims became more precise, more far-reaching.

They were received with enthusiasm by the peoples of Europe. But this policy of the President's was not a concerted strategy for war and peace, prepared and agreed upon in advance by the Allied and associated powers, but rather a projection of what Wilson firmly believed to be the desire and wish of the American people and, therefore, of all the peoples of the world able to express their will freely. It was a policy that could not stand the stress of political facts. A world returning to normalcy after an exhausting struggle soon lost interest in lofty ideals.

What happened in the councils of Europe was to happen soon in the Senate of the United States and in American public opinion. The effort had been too great. The aim had been too high. America relapsed into the state out of which President Wilson had led both himself and his country: Isolation.

When, in 1919, "the boys came home" and were demobilized, the United States entered, as far as defense was concerned, upon a period similar in many respects to the one that had preceded the World War. The annals of the Army and the Navy are filled with the description of a losing battle for officers, men, support for military study and research, for matériel and for public interest. The victory over Germany, that embodiment of militarism—the very prototype of a country with a standing army, a general staff, and extensive military establishment—by the American citizen army, created, as people liked to think, out of nothing, seemed to confirm the utter superiority of the American principle of unpreparedness.

The American public soon realized bitterly that the

14

war had not achieved its aim to end war and to make the world safe for democracy. German militarism was defeated, but the militarism of the French, British, Italian, and Japanese, and the militaristic nationalism of the newly created countries of Central Europe, and in a more remote future, a menacing Bolshevism, threatened to take its place.

A Peace-loving
yet Military Republic

ARMS CONTROL AND PEACE

The United States failure to enter the League of Nations had thwarted the high hopes staked on institutional prevention of war. Therefore, the pacifist organizations, which had been strong and effective before the war, were revived and gradually concentrated on clamoring for international disarmament. The founding of the National Council on the Limitation of Armaments was the central expression of this movement. It gained strength from the fact that leading military men, like Generals Pershing and Bliss, endorsed fully the idea of disarmament.

Since the Army had been reduced to its pre-war state, attention was now centered on the Navy, plans for the expansion of which had been endorsed even by President Wilson. The Washington Conference and the Five-Power Naval Treaty of February 6, 1922, were the result, and revealed the then-existing strategic preoccupation. Only the navies of Great Britain and Japan, and only as far as their battleships were concerned, seemed then to constitute a menace to American security. American military and public opinion easily accepted the formula of 5–5–3 agreed upon for limiting the battle fleets of the United States, Britain and Japan, and did not find fault with the far-reaching concession made to Japan in the Nine-Power Treaty of the same date which renounced any further fortification of foreign bases like the Philippines or Guam.

The initiative for and the conclusion of the Kellogg-Briand Pact of January 15, 1929, renouncing war as an instrument of national policy, was characteristic for this period of uncertain drifting before the winds of pacifist feeling and changing moods of the public. The same was true of the London Naval Reduction Treaty of April 22, 1930, which established a new relationship between the three great navies and which was practically meaningless.

Within the harassed, hardly respected, and time and again defeated military establishment, however, the lessons of a great war remained alive. The strategic thought that had directed the war effort and had been enriched by experience was inevitably applied to new circumstances. Since recent experience was unquestioningly interpreted as requiring one single theater of war, strategic planning was naturally dominated by this concept. On the other hand, expressions of isolationism so much determined public debate, legislation, congressional appropriations, and the decisions of the executive that the military could not but acknowledge this as basic national policy. Their strategic thinking was, therefore, completely oriented toward the defense of the national territory and of the Western Hemisphere. Both concepts—concentration and defense—found expression in the strategic plans drafted between the wars and in the attitudes toward the new concept of air power. New theories were readily accepted and welcomed, but their application was defeated by the stronger force of defensive thinking.

17

DEFENSIVE PLANNING

A kind of central planning agency for national strategy had existed as early as 1903, when a Joint Army and Navy Board was created by the Secretary of War and the Secretary of the Navy. Curiously enough, the Board suspended its activities in 1913, to resume them only in 1915. It was firmly reconstituted on July 25, 1919, and was then composed of the Chief of Staff of the Army, the Chief of the Operations Section and the Chief of the War Plans Division. On the Navy side sat the Chief and Assistant Chief of Naval Operations and the Chief of the Navy's War Plans Division. From both sides the Chief Air Officers were included.

To the Joint Board was added, at the same time, a Joint Planning Committee, composed of officers of the War Plans Divisions both of the Navy and the Army. In the plans developed by this committee between 1919 and 1939, American strategic thinking of that period found its most authoritative expression.

Under the influence of the recent war experience, studies were conditioned initially by the one-theater conception. Since an exhausted Europe did not seem in a position to threaten the United States, attention focused thereafter on the danger that the rising power of the Japanese empire might offer, both to the continental United States and to its Far Eastern possessions.

War Plan ORANGE, which was developed and revised several times, was a perfect reflection of the strategic theories evolved by Admiral Alfred Thayer Mahan or rather of their subsequent interpretation. An attack by Japan upon the Far Eastern possessions of the United States or against American interests was to be answered by offensive action by the Navy, designed to destroy the enemy fleet. Operations of the Army would be purely defensive. One of the Army's missions was to hold Manila Bay, where the Navy would be based. The Army's task was to include, in addition, the defense of the Panama Canal, of Hawaii, Alaska, and the western coast of the United States. Japan was to be defeated, after the destruction of its battle fleet, by isolation and harassment and by the disruption of its sea communications, so vital to the existence of the island empire. To offensive sea operations against the shipping and economic life of Japan were to be added vast air operations. Presumably it would not be necessary to invade the Japanese islands.

The views inherited from Mahan's writings had prepared the ground for newer estimation of the role and capabilities of air power. During the war, especially in the final offensive of the American Army between the Meuse and the Aisne, a first glimpse of the potentialities of air war had been gathered. The claims of the advocates of the air force were of considerable interest to the public at large, but met with a deep distrust from the heads of the Armed Services. The most passionate advocate of the air force, General William Mitchell, was assistant chief of the Air Service in the years 1921 to 1925. His convictions were strongly underlined by the results of tests made in the summer of 1921, when three ships, among them captured German battleships, were bombed off the American coast.

Mitchell's advanced views as to air power were shared by a prominent thinker on naval affairs, Admiral Sims,[1] but generally rejected by military leaders. The ensuing deep conflict went so far that Mitchell

[1] Elting E. Morison, op. cit., p. 509.

19

finally was court-martialed and removed from his positions.

Among the European powers it was Great Britain which traditionally commanded the interest of American strategic planners. Only Great Britain was in possession of a battle fleet capable of engaging the American fleet. The extended and important British island possessions in the Western Hemisphere constituted the natural bases from which to attack. Traditional thinking had it that colonial conquest and eventual attack by Britain on America were the life blood of the Empire. Quite naturally, War Plan RED, which provided defense against Great Britain alone, was reworked and modernized with greatest care, although it seemed clear to the planners, in spite of their inclination to plan for abstract military contingencies from which political considerations were as far as possible excluded, that an attack by Great Britain against the United States of America was, in the middle and late twenties, wildly unlikely. The plan, however, was interesting, since it presented one of the two alternatives of the deployment of the Navy. According to the strategic shibboleths drawn from Mahan's writings, the fleet should never be divided. President Theodore Roosevelt developed out of this axiom the extreme view that the American Navy should never be divided between the Pacific and the Atlantic Oceans. The Panama Canal, Theodore Roosevelt's treasured idea, was to be the instrument for the implementation of the doctrine of concentration. It would allow the deployment of the battleships of a "two-ocean Navy," in time of peace, in the Atlantic and the Pacific, and their concentration at shortest notice in the expected single theater of war.

Theodore Roosevelt's fixed idea found its shortest

and most moving expression in his letter of March 3, 1909, directed to President-elect Taft:

> Dear Will: One closing legacy. Under no circumstances divide the battleship fleet between the Atlantic and the Pacific Oceans prior to the finishing of the Panama Canal.[2]

On the same day the President wrote to his friend Mahan: "I am sure that the fleet will never be divided."[3]

With his writing, Admiral Alfred Thayer Mahan had influenced American strategic thinking, around the turn of the century, in an almost unbelievable way. He came to be regarded by many, especially in Europe where his writings became the leading texts of modern imperialism, as the only noteworthy American strategist. His most widely read and quoted book is *The Influence of Sea Power upon History, 1660–1783.*[4] It is actually a historian's book, with the naval wars of the seventeenth and eighteenth centuries exhaustively described and interpreted.

Mahan's views were empirical and extremely conservative. This was probably one of the main reasons why he appealed so greatly to the military profession. In addition to these qualities, his writing convinced many by its clear and incisive reasoning and a certain archaic style. The reputation of his father, General Dennis Hart Mahan, who had been one of the foremost teachers at West Point from 1832 through 1870, may also have contributed considerably to his popularity.

[2] Elting E. Morison, ed., *The Letters of Theodore Roosevelt* (Cambridge, Mass., 1952), vol. VI, p. 1543.
[3] Ibid.
[4] Boston, 1890.

Mahan's strategic theory is contained in relatively short introductory remarks to writings which otherwise are historical. In these passages he attributes to the strategic laws he believes to have discovered in wars of earlier centuries the quality of laws of nature:

> From time to time the superstructure of tactics has to be altered or wholly torn down; but the old foundations of strategy so far remain, as though laid upon a rock.[5]

His strategic theory was made a little more explicit in collections of articles and lectures and in a later book, *Naval Strategy, Compared and Contrasted with the Principles and Practices of Military Operation on Land*.[6] His thinking, both at the height of his fame, around 1905, and thereafter, was conservative, as attested by his attitude in the debate of 1905 to 1910 about the modernization of the battleship, or by his insistence that commerce raiding could never be "decisive of great issues." Thus, he failed to predict the U-boat campaigns against commerce. In justice to Mahan, however, one has to insist that, although much oriented toward the teachings of history, he was a constructive thinker, and that the interpretation later given to his writings was much more conservative than he ever intended it to be. Thus he shared the fate of another great military creator, Marshal Vauban.

In view of the doctrine that the fleet should not be divided, American planners were rather puzzled by the prospect of a simultaneous attack by RED and ORANGE, by Great Britain and Japan. The termination of the twenty-year treaty between Great Britain and Japan, in which the United States was instrumen-

[5] Op. cit., p. 88.
[6] Boston, 1911.

tal, had helped to make this contingency unlikely. The planners felt it their duty, however, to provide for it. What quickly emerged as a result of their studies was that offensive warfare by the Navy, as traditionally envisioned, could not be entertained against two powerful enemies. Therefore, an offensive undertaking in one of the two theaters would have to be combined with the defense of the other. After the defeat of one of the enemies, the offensive thrust could then be turned against the remaining foe. Thus, the "defensive-offensive" concept taught by Clausewitz, and well known to every American military thinker, would be applicable. The decision to plan for a war on two fronts was itself a dramatic change in American strategic thinking. The solution, as it emerged from ensuing study, was a revolution.

From 1935 on, the rising aggressiveness of the dictators of Italy and Germany had transformed the political scene. Germany had repudiated the military clauses of the Treaty of Versailles and embarked upon building its own military power. Italy had started its new drive for colonial conquest and brought Europe, by its aggression against Ethiopia, to the brink of a new war. In 1936 the outbreak of the Spanish Civil War and the ensuing intervention of Italy, Germany and the Soviet Union in Spain, and in 1937 the all-out invasion of China by Japan were the ominous signals of a rapidly deteriorating world situation.

The now emerging common interests of the United States and Great Britain in the Far East, in Africa and in Europe, revived the recollection of the fruitful naval co-operation between 1917 and 1918. The man now in the White House had been Under Secretary of the Navy in that crucial period. It was not difficult for him to grasp the importance of new contacts with London.

23

When, in December 1937, the Chief of Naval Operations, Admiral Leahy, dispatched Captain Royal E. Ingersoll to London for private and exploratory talks with the Admiralty, it was President Franklin D. Roosevelt in person who gave him his instructions as he set off.

The stone wall which traditionally separated strategy from policy began to give way. Emotion caused by the aggressions of Japan and Italy, and the belligerency of Germany called for bold assertion of American interests and ideals in a changing world. But the lack of material power, due to years of pacifism, antimilitarism, isolationism, and naïve belief in natural invulnerability, became now sorely apparent and intensified the growing interplay of political and military considerations.

MILITARY STRATEGY AND POLICY MEET

The breakthrough was wrought by the information, received through diplomatic channels, of growing activity of German and Italian agents, including diplomatic representatives, among the population of German and Italian origin in the Latin American countries, with Germany and Italy offering the Latin American republics help in training their armies. This struck a familiar chord, since German propaganda among Americans of German origin had been, in the United States, a matter of deepest concern during World War I. And the German offer of a treaty to Mexico, with the view of attacking the United States from a base in the Western Hemisphere, had been one of the chief factors that brought America into the war.[7]

[7] Mark Skinner Watson, *Prewar Plans and Preparations*, vol. VI of the series on *U. S. Army in World War II*, published by The War Department (Washington, 1950), p. 89.

Again the fundamental policies of the Monroe Doctrine were threatened. Again the rights of small or defenseless nations were in jeopardy. Again the threat to free trade had arisen. But what really counted was the danger to the defense of the continental United States and of the Panama Canal, which sprang from Fascist and National Socialist activities in Latin America. Suddenly people, press, and Congress began to understand that adherence to the doctrine of mere passive defense of the coasts of the United States with purely military means invited defeat. The conviction began to arise that only an active diplomacy, combined with preparedness for military action, if need be far from the territory of the United States, could answer these threats. At the outset, however, this new comprehension was strictly limited to the protection of America. Its extension to the Far East and to Europe was visualized only by a small group of political thinkers, not by the public and the press at large.

The threat to Latin America provoked a remarkable initiative by the Secretary of State, Cordell Hull. In a letter to President Roosevelt he proposed, in April 1938, to create an interdepartmental commission that would link the diplomatic service with the military. As an answer to the Axis offer to Latin American countries of military training facilities, the Foreign Service considered granting certain types of assistance to the neighbor states for the build-up of their armies and navies. It is interesting to note that in the context of this problem, it was General George Marshall who proposed financial assistance to Paraguay. To implement such complicated and unheard-of policies, the Secretary of State suggested setting up a permanent liaison committee on the level of second ranking civilian officers of the Departments of State, Navy, and War.

This initiative was readily seized upon by President Roosevelt. He, however, ordered the establishment of this standing committee on a higher level than the one that Mr. Hull had rather timidly suggested. It was to be composed of the Under Secretary of State, the Chief of Staff of the Army and the Chief of Naval Operations. The Standing Liaison Committee thus set up early in 1938 was the very first institutionalized link between the civilian and the military policy-making power, and the initiative had come from the civilians. Whereas General Marshall, who then was Assistant Chief of Staff, greatly favored this innovation, Admiral Leahy, Chief of Naval Operations, quite typically thought it unnecessary. The Committee, however, functioned primarily in the context for which it was proposed by the Department of State, namely in the improvement of the defenses of the Panama Canal and the protection of Latin America against the Axis threat.

NEW WAR PLANS

The new interest in hemispheric defense brought two absolutely unprecedented elements into American strategy. It contradicted the dissociation of power and policy which had been a golden rule except under the administration of Theodore Roosevelt, and it overcame the isolationist concept of national defense, as well as the habit of purely defensive thinking in which the military often outdid even the civilians. The challenge to the security of the hemisphere, widely overrated at that time, provided the incentive for a strategy that would come into operation before the enemy had achieved his first goals. It seemed to the Military Departments wiser to ask for congressional support in defending the South American approaches to the Panama Canal, a visibly defensive measure, than for providing resistance to German aggressiveness in faraway parts of the world.

In the field of strategic planning, the old plans BLUE, ORANGE, RED, RED-ORANGE, clearly no longer corresponded to the world situation and to the growing threat from the Axis powers and from Japan. After the September 1938 crisis in Europe, the Joint Board instructed its Planning Committee to undertake fundamentally new research.

The Committee produced an excellent comprehensive study of the strategic situation. How far the dissociation of policy and power had been overcome, at least intellectually, is evidenced by the statement in the report: "Not only must strategy be linked to policy, but it must also take cognizance of such intangibles as tradition, the spirit of the nation, and 'emotionalized public opinion.'"[8]

On the basis of this report, the Joint Army and Navy Board laid down guidelines for the future. The Planning Committee was to develop five plans, which were not to be designated in the traditional way by colors, but rather by the catchword RAINBOW and the numbers 1 to 5. RAINBOW 1, 3 and 4 started from the assumption that the United States would be at war without major allies. RAINBOW 2 and 5 assumed that the United States would be aligned with Great Britain and France. The contents of the plans are best summarized in the report of the Chief of Staff on World

[8] Kent R. Greenfield, ed., *Command Decisions*. Prepared by the Office of the Chief of Military History, Department of the Army (New York, 1959), p. 14; Chapter I by Louis Morton, "Germany First: The Basic Concept of Allied Strategy in World War II."

War II.[9] The RAINBOW plans proposed measures to achieve the following:

1. To prevent violation of the Monroe Doctrine, and to protect the United States, its possessions and its sea trade.

2. To carry out No. 1, and to sustain the authority of democratic powers in the Pacific zones.

3. To secure control of the western Pacific.

4. To afford hemispheric defense through sending U.S. task forces, if needed, to South America, and to the eastern Atlantic.

5. To achieve the purposes of 1 and 4, and to provide ultimately for sending forces to Africa or Europe in order to effect the decisive defeat of Germany or Italy or both. This plan assumed U.S. co-operation with Great Britain and France.

RAINBOW was approved by President Roosevelt on October 14, 1939. As it turned out, these plans proved helpful in the earlier phases of the war as policy guides, although some of them soon became obsolete because of the profound change in the over-all political picture.

RAINBOW 1 to 4 were not formally canceled until May 4, 1942. But only RAINBOW 5 was expanded, as early as 1940, into the comprehensive war plan, which was ready when the Japanese struck in December 1941.

The most remarkable feat in this phase of planning was that it brought forth a decision of truly historic importance. Two American traditions, both rooted in a hundred years of military thinking, stood in conflict. The dominating concern of the Navy had always been the Pacific and American interests in East Asia, where

[9] *U. S. Army in World War II*, p. 103.

28

the rules of isolationism were never strictly applied. Only the Atlantic seaboard seemed to be a true frontier of the United States, while its interests spread freely over the blue expanses of the Pacific, into the jungles of the Philippine Islands and over the hills of China. Another trend of thought, as powerful as the first, was the slogan, "Never divide the fleet," expressing the firm determination to concentrate all forces so as to deal with several enemies one by one. The conflict was resolved; the decision was made: Germany was to be defeated first.

The critical moment came when, on May 10, 1940, the "phony war" in Europe suddenly flared up into a conflagration that was soon to engulf France and threaten the very existence of Great Britain. It was now clear that the main danger to the Western Hemisphere lay in Germany's military power, and in the not too remote possibility that German National Socialism could harness well-nigh all European industrial potentialities, including manpower, to its war effort. For the naval planners it became a chief concern that the Germans should not get hold of the French and the British fleets and of French and British possessions in the Atlantic area, whereby they would be in a position to engage the United States with overwhelming naval power. The danger offered by Japan, which was not yet at war, seemed minor. And the hope prevailed that Japan's intervention in the war might be postponed.

THE FATE OF THE FAR EAST

When, therefore, in October 1940, Great Britain suggested that an American naval squadron be sent to Singapore in order to protect this crucial position

29

for common defense against Japan and to deter the Japanese from attacking toward the south, the American authorities, both Navy and Army, emphatically declined. They had made up their minds: Japan was not to be provoked, the danger lay in Europe and the Atlantic, forces were not to be scattered and divided.

The decision had, in fact, been reached earlier. On September 25, 1940, the War Plans Division had presented to the Chief of Staff a long memorandum, the fruit of close co-operation among Army, Navy and Department of State, setting out in brilliant clarity the strategic views that were to dominate coming events. The basic policy was to be recognition of Germany as the principal foe and Japan as an adversary to be fully disposed of at a later time. It is interesting to note that in spite of the determination to check Germany and to help Great Britain in its plight, there was a measure of reluctance to enter upon consultations with the British military authorities. As the report of the Chief of Staff presumes,[10] this may have been due to the fact that in the United States the election campaign was then going on, in which the candidates of both parties had asserted that no American would go abroad to fight! Two years later a huge American army was to land on the North African shores.

In early November, with the re-election of Franklin D. Roosevelt assured, the Chief of Naval Operations, Admiral Harold R. Stark, came forward with a very strong statement to the Secretary of the Navy on basic strategy in the imminent struggle. His views coincided almost completely with those put forward by the Army planners. His memorandum, which later became known as "Plan Dog" (D was then "dog" in military

[10] Ibid., p. 119.

30

parlance), while reviewing the several possible courses of action posed the question: "D. Shall we direct our efforts toward an eventual strong offensive in the Atlantic as an ally of the British, and a defensive in the Pacific?" His reply was an emphatic Yes. Stark did not think that blockade and aerial bombardment, the means favored by the British, could defeat Germany. The only certain way to victory was to defeat Germany on land. The United States would, therefore, in addition to sending naval assistance, be obliged to send large land and air forces to Europe or Africa, or both, and to participate strongly in a land offensive.[11] General Marshall fully concurred in these views.

WAR EXCLUDES POLICY

With the President re-elected and the groundwork laid, the military now needed the approval of the highest authority for their momentous decisions. The Joint Army and Navy Board instructed its Planning Committee to draft recommendations for President Roosevelt. The document was to be submitted to the President by the three highest authorities under him, the Secretaries of State, Navy and War.

And now a most significant incident occurred, which illustrated the deep division between policy and power still existing in the minds of leading persons: the heads of the Navy and War Departments approved the document as early as December; the Secretary of State, however, took exception to the idea of a joint statement. He said that he was in general agreement with the policy set out, but that, as head of a civilian de-

[11] *Command Decisions*, p. 27.

partment, he was doubtful of the propriety of his "joining in the submission to the President of a technical military statement of the present situation."[12] So it came about that one of the most momentous documents outlining American strategy, which was to guide United States policy throughout World War II, was not endorsed by the head of the State Department merely because he thought it to be outside the proper field of his civilian department.

This disagreement on a matter of form was typical of basic conceptions in total contradiction with the needs of the day. The episode, however, had a far-reaching and unexpected effect. After a conference between Secretary of War Stimson and the Secretary of State, Cordell Hull, it was agreed that co-operation in shaping basic strategy was necessary. The three heads of department would meet, henceforward, each Tuesday "re National Defense matters."[13] Roosevelt, in turn, evidently prompted by these developments, summoned to the White House on January 16, 1941, for the first time what later came to be called the War Council. It consisted of the President, the Secretaries of State, War and Navy, and the Chiefs of Staff of the two Services, and it was to meet, under the chairmanship of the President, to discuss all matters of strategic importance.

But when the United States was actually engaged in war, President Roosevelt followed the earlier precedent by impressing on everyone the concept that war had now superseded policy. He liked to be considered and referred to as Commander-in-Chief instead of as

[12] *U. S. Army in World War II*, p. 123.
[13] *The Memoirs of Cordell Hull* (New York, 1948), vol. II, pp. 1109 f., 1570 f.

President. After the day of Pearl Harbor, he excluded the Secretary of State from the Council—a determination by then deeply regretted and disapproved of by Mr. Cordell Hull, that civilian gentleman of late so hesitant to join in strategic decisions.[14] And throughout the war, the chief officer in the cabinet responsible for the conduct of the foreign policy of his government was never to go to the international conferences, which the President and the military chiefs attended. He was not in the White House when the British Prime Minister conferred with the President, and Roosevelt never informed him of what had been decided. This fact is too striking, and falls too much into the pattern of agreed traditional strategic thinking to be explained merely by an unpleasant personal relationship between the President and the Secretary of State.

President Roosevelt used the occasion of the first meeting of his War Council to make a statement on national strategy. He concentrated, typically enough, on the defensive problems that the situation in the Far East presented. This statement of January 16, 1941, was soon found inadequate as a guide for the effort then beginning to bring decisive help to Britain and to prepare the United States for war. Following new instructions from the President, a comprehensive program was set up, later to be known as the Victory Program. It was sent to the White House on September 25, 1941.

After the extensive staff work for this program had begun, it soon became apparent that national strategy was still "too nebulous" to provide a firm basis for a total mobilization of the nation's power, so the Gen-

14 Ibid.

eral Staff itself then drew up a basic document describing strategy for the coming war. The most significant points of this statement were: resist with all means Axis penetration in the Western Hemisphere; convey to Japan the determination of the United States to take positive action; avoid major military and naval commitments in the Far East at this time; the principal theater of operations is Europe, but other possible theaters of operations may later appear desirable; the defeat of the potential enemies is primarily dependent on the defeat of Germany.

The course of the war, including the war aims, were described in rather laconic terms:

1st Phase (until M-Day or when hostilities begin).
Objective: Insure delivery of supplies to the British Isles and provide munitions for other nations fighting the Axis, in order to preclude a diminution of their war effort, and concurrently prepare United States forces for active participation in the war.
2nd Phase (M-Day until prepared for final offensive action).
Objective: Prepare the way for eventual defeat of Germany by active participation as associate of Great Britain and other nations fighting the Axis powers.
Final Phase. Objective: Total defeat of Germany.

These were the strategic concepts included in the Victory Program and its annexes. On the methods and the order of urgency, however, the Army and Navy did not completely agree. The compromise formula they found may be summarized as follows: since ground force strength was limited, full use should be made of naval and air resources against Germany. The

Navy felt that greater numbers of men might not be as potent as machines and blockade. But, since air and naval attack admittedly could not defeat Germany, land strength for the ultimate battle on the continent of Europe would have to be provided.

The war aims as stated in the Victory Program may be summarized as follows:

1. Preservation of the integrity of the whole Western Hemisphere;

2. Prevention of the disruption of the British Commonwealth;

3. Prevention of further extension of Japanese dominion;

4. Eventual re-establishment in Europe and Asia of a balance of power furthering political stability in those regions and future security of the United States;

5. Establishment, as far as practicable, of regimes favorable to economic freedom and individual liberty.[15]

While the Victory Program was still on the loom, the war aims had been given a dramatic (although general and non-committal) expression by those in the highest authority. In their common declaration of August 14, 1941, later to be called the Atlantic Charter, and sanctioned on January 1, 1942, in the Declaration by United Nations, President Roosevelt and Prime Minister Churchill had, in eight points, described their intentions and the meaning of the war. The paragraph that comes nearest to a declaration on strategy and war aims reads as follows:

Sixth, after the final destruction of the Nazi tyranny, they hope to establish a peace which will afford to all

15 *U. S. Army in World War II*, p. 356.

35

nations the means of dwelling in safety within their own boundaries, and which will afford assurance that all the men in all the lands may live out their lives in freedom from fear and want.

III

Thought and Experience
in World War II

When, on December 7, 1941, war came to the United
States, the basic strategy set up in the RAINBOW
plans remained as immutable "as if built upon a rock."
There was no wavering as to the primary object of
the war: the defeat of Germany. The plan to deter
but not provoke Japan had failed, but the decision to
remain on the defensive in the Pacific and the Far
East was upheld. Its wisdom was underlined by the
shocking fact that the battle fleet in the Pacific had
for all practical purposes been crippled. The defense
of the Philippines and of Guam, which as early as
November 1938, the Joint Planning Committee had
considered not to be a vital American interest, became
a mere holding action. Since no fleet was to operate
in the near future from Manila Bay, the Island of
Luzon could readily be abandoned. How casual the
President was about these positions was apparent in
his statement on strategy in the War Council of December 16, 1941, when he ruled that "the Commander
of the Asiatic Fleet would have discretionary authority
as to how long he could remain based in the Philippines and to his direction of withdrawal—to the East
or to Singapore." It is, moreover, an example, very

reminiscent of President Wilson's thinking, of how in the mind of an American President policy ends after the beginning of war. A decision of the utmost politico-strategic importance, whether the "Asiatic" fleet should join the Allies by steaming into Singapore and participate in the defense of British, Dutch and French possessions, or join the U.S. fleet at Pearl Harbor, or sail to the Panama Canal or elsewhere, was left to the discretion of the naval commander on the spot! War is war, the Government had to abdicate . . .

The originally purely defensive strategy against Japan was, before long, to show certain offensive aspects. Since the Japanese had not succeeded in destroying the American aircraft carriers and had left the base facilities at Pearl Harbor practically intact, the Navy was soon able to engage in a war of harassment. It was not Mahan's strategy. It was a strategy of the weak, reminding one very much of Britain's peripheral strategy against Germany. Harassment reached its first peak in General Doolittle's raid against Tokyo, conducted from the aircraft carrier *Hornet* on April 18, 1942. The raid also helped to bolster American morale at a time when the Philippines were falling. Soon after, the aircraft carriers engaged the Japanese fleet in two defensive battles. In May 1942, in the Battle of the Coral Sea, they defeated the escort of the Japanese transports which intended to land their troops at Port Moresby, and in the Battle of Midway in June, defeated the Japanese fleet protecting the troopships headed toward these islands.

GERMANY FIRST

The dominant aim, however, remained the defeat of Germany. Throughout the years 1942 and 1943 the

American High Command had to struggle for this objective. The records of the meetings of the Combined Chiefs of Staff, which directed the combined military effort of the United States, Britain and their Allies, the records of the conversations between Franklin D. Roosevelt and Winston Churchill, their correspondence, even the meetings of the American Joint Chiefs of Staff, give proof of one issue overshadowing all others: The Americans were determined to defend the implementation of their basic strategic concept—the defeat, by one massive onslaught by land forces, of the armies of the principal foe—against advocates of any other course of action.

The occasion for conflicts over this basic strategic concept was not slow in presenting itself. For the American planners, the obvious course was to build up troop strength in the British Isles in order to secure that essential position, and later to launch an attack from there against Western Europe. These plans, known under the code names BOLERO-ROUNDUP (build-up in Britain, peripheral raids, full-scale invasion in 1943) and SLEDGEHAMMER (a limited landing in Western Europe in 1942 in order to ease the pressure on the Soviet Union) came immediately under fire from the British. Britain was more interested in an early landing in North Africa, for obvious reasons, and was secretly committed to postponing the all-out invasion, in the conviction that it should be undertaken only when overwhelming strength was available and Germany further weakened by the air offensive.

The decision to undertake in 1942 the landing in North Africa, later to be known under the code name TORCH, was made by President Roosevelt and Prime Minister Churchill, against strong resistance from the

American Chiefs of Staff, General Marshall and Admiral King. It is one of the important instances of the war when President Roosevelt overruled his military advisers, and one of the relatively few occasions when exclusively political considerations determined military planning.

The motives were clear: Roosevelt feared that Stalin was quite capable of coming to terms with Hitler if America did not undertake military action at the earliest possible moment. To the empirical American mind the events of 1917, when Russia was pushed out of the war, had the value of a precedent that could not be ignored. Roosevelt shared the British hope that France could be brought back into the war; he understood the need to bolster up the Allies' position in the Middle East; he firmly believed, much more than his military advisers, in the effectiveness of bombing Germany. But he had a congressional election at hand, and, in any case, he did not really think in military dimensions. And there may be some truth in the rather frivolous remark General Marshall made in 1957 to Admiral Samuel Eliot Morison, which the latter relates in his book *Strategy and Compromise*, to the effect that he had learned in 1942 the great lesson that "in wartime the politicians have to do *something* important every year."[1]

CONFLICTS WITH THE BRITISH

When, after endless haggling, the decision to land in North Africa was finally taken, the difference between American and British strategic thinking immediately reappeared. The British, and some Americans in London, accustomed to or freshly acquainted with

[1] Boston, 1958, p. 38.

the concept of peripheral warfare, whose chief proponent was Churchill, proposed a bold thrust into the Mediterranean, with troop landings in Algeria and Tunisia. Admiral Cunningham went as far as to suggest steaming with the fleet right into Bizerta. Yet, neither General Marshall nor Admiral King, could visualize any other solution than to begin at the far end, in Morocco, to secure space for army deployment, ports and railroads and then to work their way east. When General Eisenhower, who was to command the operation, was asked for his opinion, he proposed in typical fashion some sort of compromise—a lot in Morocco and a little in Algeria.

Much deeper, much more complex were the strategic decisions to be taken once the southern coast of the Mediterranean was secured. As the Americans had feared and the British had certainly planned, once they were committed to this theater there was no way of getting out again. The decision to attack in the northern Mediterranean, therefore, was not even necessary. It had been taken care of by events.

The idea of attacking Germany and Italy from the south was a British and Churchillean concept; the implementation was classical American strategy. In August 1943 the capture of Sicily forced the capitulation of Italy, and in September the Italian mainland was invaded. Once a front was established across the peninsula, it was pushed, by frontal attacks, across mountains and valleys, until it bogged down. The only diversion attempted—the landing at Anzio on January 22, 1944—while initiated successfully, was not exploited by the over-cautious commander. Once again, true to the tradition of leaving decisions of the highest strategic importance to the commander in the field, no one thought to give orders for methods of exploit-

41

ing the surprise of the enemy, which could easily have led to the capture of Rome.

Because of their commitment to the frontal assault in Italy, the American military leaders opposed every additional diversion of forces from the final supreme attack, OVERLORD, planned by then for the summer of 1944 against the coasts of France. The arguments and proposals from the British side for other operations in the Mediterranean area—such as the capture of Rhodes, the opening of the Dardanelles, bringing Turkey into the war, landings on the Yugoslavian coast —and American resistance to them on the ground that they would only mean further postponement of OVERLORD, consumed the long series of war conferences, from Casablanca to Teheran, and fill volumes of records, memoirs, and critical historical works.

All these extremely complex negotiations and recriminations among the Allies, complicated as they were by the enigmatic attitude of the Soviet Union, bear ample witness to the basic facts: the American strategists were deeply disturbed by the attitudes of the British, and this disturbance only served to confirm their deep traditional distrust, still an integral part of American folklore. The mere fact that policy—the vision of distant aims in distant lands, concern with final settlements after the war—were constantly in the minds of the British leaders, both political and military, constantly and visibly influencing their strategic thinking and planning, deeply divided them from their American opposite numbers. General Marshall, Admiral King and General Arnold were exclusively concerned with defeating by means of overwhelming forces the German armies in Western Europe. Whoever, therefore, brought politics into play, as the British constantly did, simply seemed to be an enemy of early and total victory. The history of conflicts within the Alliance shows, as the war went on, a remarkable reinforcement of traditional American strategic thinking despite the changing patterns of modern technological world-wide war.

President Roosevelt's personal attitude toward the problem of policy and war after Pearl Harbor is a subject of controversy. Did he draw in his mind a line between his responsibility as head of state and nominal commander-in-chief, assigning to the military the over-all aims to be achieved, and leaving strictly military decisions to the Joint Chiefs of Staff? Or did he interpret his role as commander-in-chief in a more extensive way, suggesting specific courses of action or overruling military decisions?

The generally accepted view is that Roosevelt relied on General Marshall's advice and simply defended, in the Allied councils, the strategy worked out by the military authority. A study by Kent Roberts Greenfield, the Chief Historian of the Department of the Army from 1946 to 1958, however, shows that the situation was much more complex.[2] He lists twenty-two cases where the President decided against the advice or over the protests of his military advisers, and thirteen cases of probable military initiatives of the President. It is evident that Franklin Delano Roosevelt's attitude toward military strategy is closer to Abraham Lincoln's deep involvement with the conduct of the Civil War than to Woodrow Wilson's attitude toward World War I. For Roosevelt his position of commander-in-chief became the full expression of the powers of the President in time of national crisis. Since he had dominated the scene for nearly ten years, he

[2] *American Strategy in World War II: A Reconsideration* (Baltimore, 1963), pp. 49 ff.

would dominate it, unquestioned, throughout the war, until his death.

Yet, his conduct of the war was typical of the traditional American outlook, and shaped by it. His was the political responsibility in the widest sense. He would set up the armies and navies and equip them. He would handle the complicated relationship with the Allies. He was convinced that he alone could keep together the strange alliance between Stalin's Soviet Union, Churchill's British Empire, and the United States. He would handle the difficult problems of defeated France. He would not hesitate to impose military decisions when he thought they were vital to these specific aims. Yet, exactly as his Joint Chiefs of Staff gave specific and detailed instructions in certain cases, and left the most fantastic freedom to the commander in the field in others, the President interfered with minor military details when they were related to over-all preparedness or the relationship between Allies, but for the operations themselves always tried to uphold the traditional concept that they were a matter for the military.

Since Roosevelt died before the conclusion of the war and before the most far-reaching politico-military decisions had to be taken, we will never know how far he would have intervened in the conduct of the final operations, which shaped the political map of present-day Europe. President Truman, for many obvious reasons, took the traditional attitude that a wide gap separates policy from the immediate conduct of the war.

UNCONDITIONAL SURRENDER

The force of tradition in American strategic thinking and the power of American folklore are illustrated by an incident that was later inflated by journalists, politicians and historians until it reached extraordinary proportions—unconditional surrender.

When, on January 26, 1943, at the end of the Casablanca Conference, President Roosevelt spoke informally to the press, he obviously could not disclose the secret military decisions which had been reached. In order to have something impressive to say, it occurred to him that he might announce that he and Prime Minister Churchill were agreed that the only terms on which they would deal in future with any Axis government or Axis faction were "unconditional surrender." Churchill, who was present, expressed agreement. He stated in his *War Memoirs,* that both before and during the conference he had meditated on the possibility of a declaration to the effect that the war would be waged mercilessly until the unconditional surrender of Germany and Japan. Italy was intentionally left out in the hope that it might soon defect to the Allies. The problem was discussed at the conference, but no agreement was reached. It came, therefore, as a surprise to those initiated, when Roosevelt used the term "unconditional surrender" to the journalists. Roosevelt was, as he later pointed out, surprised himself that he had used the word.

He, of course, was referring to the note that General Ulysses S. Grant of Civil War fame had scribbled in reply to a message from the commandant of Fort Donelson, on February 16, 1862: "No terms except an unconditional and immediate surrender can be accepted." This phrase is probably known to most American schoolboys. It is part of American folklore, for it seems to express perfectly the national ideal of "toughness" and the longing of the American mind for "all or nothing." Roosevelt used it without giving further thought to its immediate implications, except that he probably thought of excluding the possibility of a "stab-in-the-back" legend being developed, in analogy to World War I, by the Germans at a later date. Churchill, admirably familiar with the history of the Civil War, was certainly delighted to hear such a classic slogan.

Later the President tried to give a deeper political meaning to his words. In an address in Washington, on February 12, 1943, he referred to attempts by the Axis powers to divide the Alliance and to seek separate deals with the members. To these attempts, which he scorned utterly, he opposed the determination that only unconditional surrender would serve the Alliance's high purposes.

It will be difficult even for later historians to decide whether the introduction of the historic phrase into the war helped or damaged the cause of the Allies or whether it had no consequences whatsoever. However considered, it gave admirable expression to an essential of American strategic thinking at the time, that war is to be waged without a political aim in mind.

When, on June 6, 1944, Operation OVERLORD finally was launched, American strategy had triumphed. The great thrust to defeat the German armies was to be conducted with overwhelming might until the aim —unconditional surrender of what remained of the once-powerful German war machine—was achieved.

NO POLITICS

Time and again, however, controversies between the single-minded conduct of the war to the exclusion of political considerations, as prosecuted by General Ei-

senhower, and the more flexible approach advocated by the British, as personified by Winston
Churchill, flared up. The most significant episode is
the discussion over Operation ANVIL, the landing of
two armies in the south of France—which on August
15, 1944, was brilliantly performed under the code
name DRAGOON.

ANVIL had been decided upon as early as November 1943, at the Teheran Conference, as an operation
integrally related to the landing in Normandy. After
the successful landing across the Channel, the British
suggested canceling the supporting operation from the
south and using the means thus made available for an
operation in the Adriatic. The American military leaders sharply opposed this change for reasons that can
easily be imagined.

More interesting is the attitude of President Roosevelt, because it throws light on his basic thinking. He
refused even to consider proposals—which we might
call proposals of higher strategy—for such plans as
widening the pincer movement from one restricted to
France to one attacking the German armies from the
south and the rear, or penetrating ahead of the Russians into southeastern Europe. With regard to the
all-important build-up for Operation OVERLORD, he
said in a message to Churchill: I "consider this definitely Eisenhower's responsibility." Roosevelt, however, did acknowledge being swayed by the politician's
reflections when he wrote Prime Minister Churchill:
"Finally, for purely political considerations over here,
I should never survive even a slight setback in Overlord if it were known that fairly large forces had been
diverted to the Balkans."[3]

[3] Winston S. Churchill, *Triumph and Tragedy*, vol. VI of *The
Second World War* (Boston, 1953), pp. 721, 723.

Throughout the campaign in Europe the dominant ideas that had shaped American strategy in World War I continued to operate and were expressed again and again. The volumes of war memoirs and of historians' criticism or advocacy of each single command decision of this most written about period of our times are full of them. We may sum up the situation in the words of General Omar N. Bradley:

> I could see no political advantages accruing from the capture of Berlin that would offset the need for quick destruction of the German army on our front. As soldiers we looked naively on this British inclination to complicate the war with political foresight and non-military objectives.[4]

And the official historian of General Eisenhower's Headquarters, Forrest C. Pogue, relates that the decision as to whether Berlin was to be taken by the U. S. Army was never even discussed in Washington, but left entirely to the discretion of the commander in the field.[5]

Strikingly similar concepts had been expressed in connection with the Civil War, when General Schofield sharply criticized Sherman's March to the Sea as not at all consistent with the "dictates of established principles in the conduct of a military campaign." The whole disdain for politico-military concepts was expressed in his words: "It was, perhaps, not *war* but rather *statesmanship* upon which Sherman was about to enter."[6]

[4] *A Soldier's Story* (New York, 1951), pp. 531–37, 544.
[5] *Command Decisions*, p. 381.
[6] John M. Schofield, op. cit., p. 311.

ROADS TO TOKYO

The war against Japan had not been conducted entirely along the defensive lines originally envisaged by the RAINBOW plans. The American Navy had recovered much sooner than had originally been expected, certainly much sooner than the Japanese strategic planners had counted on, from the blow of Pearl Harbor. Japanese troop landings on Palau and Midway had been prevented. Australia of necessity had to be protected as the future springboard for the strike against Japan. The law that an initial engagement of force naturally produces further commitments came into play. The colossal war effort of the American nation produced more combatants than could usefully be engaged in Africa and Europe; the only limits to their deployment lay in shipping and landing craft. The concentrated war effort in Europe had to be secure against the danger of any attack against the continental United States and the arsenal which she had become, a security to be bought by pinning down the Japanese forces. This was successfully undertaken under the inspiring and imaginative leadership of General Douglas MacArthur.

When, in December 1944, the defeat of Germany was imminent, the Combined Chiefs of Staff in Cairo decided that bases should be obtained from which to force the unconditional surrender of Japan. In this decision the whole strategy pursued by the American High Command from the resumption of the offensive was summed up.

In planning the defeat of Japan, much greater weight than in the case of Germany was laid on the use of air power. As early as his first War Council on

January 16, 1941, President Roosevelt, in orally summing up his strategic directives, had instructed the Navy to consider the possibility of bombing attacks against Japanese cities.

Roosevelt was a strong believer in air power, as he was in naval power. After he had received, in October 1938, the reports of his ambassador to Paris on the deep concern existing in both France and Britain about the growth of German air power, and later the reports on the destruction and loss of life caused in the Spanish Civil War and in China by aerial bombings, he began to concentrate his attention on these methods. It was partly the appeal of the concentrated destructive power represented by modern airplanes that led the President away from the earlier American concept of Just Warfare—limitation of warfare to the combatant troops and the exclusion of the non-combatant civilian population—but he had another, stronger incentive. He suddenly came to visualize a war that might be won without engaging American armies in land combat, an idea always deeply disturbing to American popular opinion, to the vocal "liberal sector" of the people, to the Congress and, therefore, to the politician in the White House. He wondered whether America could not expand its production of heavy bombers and sell them to France and Britain in such numbers that they would be able to defeat Hitler without American armed intervention.[7]

To be sure, such ideas could not be carried to their extreme limits. Congress could be depended on to object violently to the idea of letting the Europeans have advanced American weapons. Furthermore, the military planners demonstrated that what at that time was called a balanced force, a force able to take and de-

[7] *U. S. Army in World War II,* pp. 131 ff.

fend the advanced air bases needed for the bombers of that period, was the right tool for victory.

The Air Corps had been enormously expanded. It achieved—after May 10, 1940, with full congressional support—the foremost position in planning and procurement. By its sheer weight the Air Service soon grew to be the equal of the Navy and Army. In March 1942 its Chief, General Arnold—in spite of the still existing equality of ground and air forces under the Army Chief of Staff—was given equality with the chief officers of Army and Navy, in the Joint Chiefs of Staff, the Combined Chiefs of Staff, and the whole realm of strategic planning.

Long before the Cairo decision the advance toward Japan in preparation for a final attack had commenced. The first steps were occupation of Guadalcanal in August 1942, the Battle of the Bismarck Sea in March 1943, the offensive through New Guinea from southeast to northwest in 1943 and 1944, and the assault on Tarawa in the Central Pacific in November 1943.

The year 1943 was filled with dissensions about the nature of the strategy to be applied in the assault. General MacArthur could visualize no other approach than that of taking one island after the other, working his way up along the axis New Guinea—Mindanao—Luzon, thence to Formosa and the Chinese mainland, and finally to Japan. The Navy and Air Force advocated other courses. It rather looked as if General Marshall and Admiral King had been infected, in their frequent contacts with the British military and with Winston Churchill, with unorthodox thinking; they decided on the "leapfrogging" approach. The heavily defended strongholds of the Japanese—for instance Rabaul, where at the end of the war a garrison of

100,000 was found—were by-passed. Less well-defended islands were taken and converted into air and submarine bases.

On October 3, 1944, the Joint Chiefs of Staff finally put an end to the long drawn out and heated controversy as to whether MacArthur's systematic approach or the Navy's more daring solution should prevail. MacArthur proposed to climb up the ladder of islands and finally take the northernmost island of the Philippines, Luzon. He was moved by two main considerations: He wanted a wide and firm land base before the invasion of Japan, and he felt honor-bound to liberate the whole of the Philippines—which meant taking the capital city, Manila—at the earliest possible date. The Navy wanted simply to secure a foothold in the south of the Philippines and thence drive to Formosa, Hongkong and the Ryukyu Islands. At the same time they stressed the importance of a lateral approach across the Central Pacific and along the Bonin Islands.

MacArthur's views prevailed. He landed in January 1945 in northern Luzon. Manila was taken on February 25. In a parallel, lateral move, the Navy continued its amphibious operations directed to the securing of airfields on the approaches to Japan. In April 1945 Iwo Jima in the Volcano Islands was taken and Okinawa invaded. The troops on the latter island, however, resisted until July, by which time no fewer than 110,000 of its garrison and population were dead.

MAHAN AT LEYTE

Before these events took place, a remarkable example of strategic flexibility was given by the American command. According to the existing plans, MacArthur was to secure the southernmost island of the

Philippines, Mindanao, and later the smaller island of Leyte. No sooner was the weakness of the Japanese air arm on the Philippines discovered than the Joint Chiefs of Staff decided to authorize the commander in the field to by-pass Mindanao and to strike first against Leyte. The landing in Leyte Gulf began on October 20, 1944. It drew a formidable reaction from the Japanese, who tried to attack the landing forces with two fleets, practically all that remained of the Imperial Navy. In addition, in the north, a weak decoy force appeared with the intention of distracting American forces.

In the ensuing naval battle of Leyte Gulf, an incident occurred that illustrates how traditional strategic thinking and training may shape command decisions when they have to be taken under the strain of combat. In the Battle of the Philippine Sea, in June 1944, Admiral Raymond Spruance had missed an opportunity to destroy the Japanese aircraft carrier force because he stuck to his main and probably more important mission of covering the amphibious assault. This had, however, been considered opposed to the strategic doctrine, attributed to Admiral Mahan, that the principal object in war is always "to destroy the enemy's fleet." Before the operation against Leyte, the commanders were, therefore, reminded in their orders of what was thought to be the Mahan doctrine. This moved Admiral Halsey to pursue the weak Japanese decoy force far to the north, almost forgetting his chief mission in connection with the landing. The mistake created a dangerous situation, although it did not lead to disaster. The Japanese main force, after engaging small United States forces, retired, probably discouraged by the destruction of the southernmost force in

Surigao Strait. But the case illustrates the working of strategic shibboleths.

Another shibboleth of the time was Mahan's axiom, "never divide the fleet." For Mahan, historian and strategist, this belonged to the conceptual framework of his views on world strategy. The same holds true for his faithful disciple, President Theodore Roosevelt. But in the hands of later naval commanders it had been transferred in a most schematic way to the realm of tactics, with the result that in World War II the tactical commanders in many a case did not dare to detach parts of the fleet in order to deal with weak enemy forces.

FROM JUST WAR TO OBLITERATION BOMBING

With the Philippines secured and airfields in Tinian, Saipan and Guam ready for use by the B-29 bombers, systematic bombing of Japan began in November 1944. The operations started with high altitude attacks, planned as precision daylight bombings of the aircraft and related industries. It soon became apparent that these bombings were less than effective. The widely scattered and barely identifiable small targets could not be singled out and the precision of high altitude bombing was only relative.

The air commander, General Curtis E. LeMay, therefore decided on a change in air strategy. He engaged in night raids, supplanting high explosive with incendiary bombs, and took to systematic obliteration of Japanese cities. The most spectacular raid was one on the night of March 9–10, 1945, in which 2000 tons of incendiary bombs were dropped on Tokyo, destroying 250,000 houses, making a million homeless and killing 85,000 persons in the ensuing fire storm. Approximately fifty Japanese cities, among them Osaka and Kobe, were severely damaged by obliteration bombing. (In addition, many other targets were attacked by precision bombing with high explosives.) These tactics were highly successful, since the lightly built residential areas of Japanese cities were an easy prey to incendiaries. The widely dispersed system of small factories and shops that contributed to aircraft production was disrupted and destroyed along with the dwellings of the workers.

Secretary of War Henry Stimson had insisted that the city of Kyoto should be spared, and his orders were carefully respected. The case is worthy of notice, since it is one of the few occasions where cultural interests prevailed over the "necessities of war."

The choice of bombing procedure, a strategic decision of high importance, had been left, in typical fashion, to the local commander. The concepts of just war, of attack against military objectives exclusively, sparing non-combatants, widely proclaimed at the beginning of the war as the essence of American strategy in opposition to the strategy of dictators and tyrants, was jettisoned by a military commander.

LeMay's decision was not questioned, and the explanation is simple. The High Command was exclusively concerned with military matters, and very much so. It went to great lengths to consider and decide questions of detail in matters of operations—for instance, whether to land first in Mindanao or Leyte. But the military planners refused to consider—nay, it did not occur to them to consider—matters of morality, policy, final aims, future evolutions—in brief, matters of high strategy in the true sense. These were and remained the province of political authority, namely the President. The President, in turn, was not concerned with these matters so long as military operations were being conducted, unless they were completely separated from them.

The fear that "politics" might interfere with war was overwhelming. This attitude was reinforced by a semantic imprecision, namely, what is meant in American parlance by "politics." In this frame of reference it means congressional meddling with military matters, patronage, favoritism, graft—connotations nourished by the history of the Civil War.

The sound distrust of any intrusion of politics of this kind into the conduct of military operations destroyed, along the way, a totally different and valuable concept of politics in war: it reinforced a tendency to exclude considerations of high policy, such as the application of moral principles in the conduct of operations, the formulation of war aims, and the vision of a world after the war, from what was considered the province of warfare.

LANDING IN JAPAN?

By the spring of 1945 the successful airmen and with them the Navy had begun to contemplate the possibility that blockade and continued aerial obliteration bombing might force Japan to surrender, as envisioned in the RAINBOW plans. The Army, however, remained firmly committed to the concept of a powerful landing on the Japanese islands in order to destroy, in a final battle, the Emperor's armies. Troops and shipping needed for the final assault began to concentrate in the Pacific area.

On June 18, 1945, President Truman, at a meeting of the War Council, approved the Joint Chiefs of Staff's plan for the invasion of Japan. By November, General

MacArthur was to land on the southern island of Kyu-shu. Once the airfields were secured, he would invade, early in 1946, the main island of Honshu. The war might then be brought to an end toward the end of 1946. Allied casualties, it was estimated, would reach a million, Japanese casualties would be much higher.

All the planners at the highest level naturally knew about project MANHATTAN, but very few seemed to realize what was to be expected of it and when it would yield the anticipated results. The possibility of using S–1 (the atomic bomb) as a warning to Japan was brought up by John J. McCloy at the President's War Council of June 18. The civilian advisers present included Secretary of War Henry L. Stimson and As-sistant Secretary John J. McCloy. The latter records that someone suggested, almost casually, when the meeting was already breaking up, that serious atten-tion should be given to an attempt to end the war by political means, and he remarks: "Now this incident indicates that at the time everyone was so intent on winning the war by military means that the intro-duction of political considerations was almost acci-dental."[8]

The idea of a political step, however, appealed to President Truman, who invited Henry Stimson to draft suggestions. On July 2, 1945, Stimson addressed a memorandum to the President[9] in which he proposed a stern warning to Japan and an invitation to surren-der, which was later, on July 26, released as the Decla-ration of the Potsdam Conference.

News of the successful explosion of the first atomic

[8] *The Challenge to American Foreign Policy* (Cambridge, Mass., 1953), pp. 42 f.
[9] Henry L. Stimson and McGeorge Bundy, *On Active Serv-ice in Peace and War* (New York, 1947), p. 623.

bomb in the desert of New Mexico had in the meantime reached the President and his advisers at Potsdam. At the same time news of an intercepted exchange of telegrams between the Japanese Foreign Minister and the Japanese Ambassador in Moscow had reached them as well. The gist of the exchange was that Japan was seeking to end the war through the good offices of the Soviet Union. In the Foreign Minister's instructions to his Ambassador it was expressly stated that "unconditional surrender is the only obstacle to peace." This important piece of intelligence, a hint of how the war might be brought to an early conclusion, was never even considered. President Truman took no steps in Potsdam except to release the pre-arranged declaration. The war took its course.

BOMBS ON HIROSHIMA AND NAGASAKI

President Truman decided, upon the unanimous advice of his highest military and civilian advisers, and great encouragement from Churchill, to use the bomb if the Japanese did not act in response to the Potsdam Declaration. Orders were issued at once to the Air Force. The Air Force had been training, for some time, a special bomber group then stationed on the island of Tinian, in preparation for an eventual dropping of the atomic bomb. The commander of the U. S. Army Strategic Air Force was instructed, on July 25, 1945, to "deliver its first special bomb as soon as weather will permit visual bombing after about 3 August 1945 on one of the targets: Hiroshima, Kokura, Niigata and Nagasaki . . ."[10] August 3rd was assumed to be the

[10] *The Army Air Forces in World War II*, vol. V entitled *The Pacific: Matterhorn to Nagasaki, June 1944 to August 1945*, Wesley Frank Craven and James Lea Cate, eds. (Chicago, 1953); reproduction opposite p. 697.

date by which the Japanese could have offered surrender under the terms of the Potsdam Declaration
of July 26. No further decision of the President or additional order to the local air commander was necessary. When on August 3 the President, then on the
way back to America aboard the cruiser *Augusta,* did
not rescind the order previously given, the bomb had
to be dropped. On August 6 the weather seemed suf-
ficiently favorable to the local commander; Hiroshima
was bombed.

The second bomb was technically ready on August
9. The Air Force's orders read to continue the operation until otherwise directed. Since the local commander was informed by his meteorologists that a spell
of bad weather was to be expected, he moved up the
date from the day originally planned, August 11, to
August 9. The first choice target this time was Kokura, but weather conditions and a shortage of fuel
prompted the commander of the airplane carrying the
bomb to drop it on the second possible target assigned
to him, Nagasaki.

Immediately after the first bomb had fallen on Hiroshima, a great propaganda effort had been set up
to inform the Japanese people of the terrifying fact,
by leaflets and broadcasts. The people were urged to
petition the Emperor to finish the war. But long before there was sufficient time for the government,
much less the people, to react, the second bomb had
fallen on Nagasaki. On August 15, 1945, the Emperor
broadcast to his people and troops that the war was
ended.

The events of July and August 1945, preceding the
decision to use the bomb and its actual dropping, are
further instances of by now well-known strategic
thinking and procedure. The decision-makers concen-

59

trate, since they are engaged in war, on military aspects, almost to the exclusion of any considerations of policy. And the military aspects are dominated by two viewpoints: end the war by destroying the enemy's power to resist; end the war quickly by a display of overwhelming power, so that American casualties may be reduced.

Political means, even when suggested, even when within easy reach, are neglected. Once the military decision is taken, it remains for the military commander on the spot to put it into effect. His is the final word. Even decisions that finally may turn out to be of the utmost political importance are left to him; the political authority has abdicated in his favor.

IV

Natural Science and Strategy

The unleashing of the energies contained in the nucleus of the atom was the event that marked the turning point of strategic thinking in America and, later, radiating outward, in the whole world. "The classic art of manipulating military power locally in war has been expanded to become a science of erecting and exercising that power on a global scale in contest with antagonistic forces even in time of relative peace."[1] Hidden in the experience of World War II lay the beginnings of this new era of strategic thought. A whole chain of events, some of them seemingly insignificant, led from earlier American thought to the full unfolding of strategic theory and strategic expertise. The more significant events of this chain can be discerned and listed.

A meeting on October 11, 1939, may be considered one of them. On that day, the economist Alexander Sachs was received by President Franklin Delano Roosevelt at the White House. Sachs presented a letter that Albert Einstein had signed on August 2, 1939.[2]

[1] Wesley W. Posvar (Colonel, U. S. Air Force), *Strategy Expertise and National Security* (mimeographed; Cambridge, Mass., 1964), p. 38.
[2] Richard G. Hewlett and Oscar E. Anderson, Jr., *The New World, 1939/1946*, vol. I entitled *A History of the United States Atomic Energy Commission* (University Park, Pa., 1962), pp. 15 ff.

Earlier in the year the physicist Enrico Fermi had drawn the attention of the Navy authorities to the potentialities of nuclear fission. In spite of great interest, especially from the Naval Research Laboratory, bureaucratic hindrances prevented the Navy from taking any active steps. Now, a letter had been drafted by Leo Szilard and Eugene Wigner, in consultation with the great old man, in the hope of warning the government of the new source of energy that almost certainly would spring from the simultaneous work of scientists in Britain, Germany, France, Denmark, Sweden, Norway, and the United States.

A great many of the men working in American universities in the field of uranium research were European physicists who had been compelled to leave their respective homes and laboratories by the anti-semitism practiced in Germany and Italy. They were privy to the basic research undertaken in Germany, which had exercised such a deep influence on the rapid development of nuclear physics since the discovery of the neutron by Sir James Chadwick in 1932. They could not but conclude, from their knowledge of that research and the fast progress they were themselves making, that Germany might in the near future produce a chain reaction in a mass of uranium and thus soon be in possession of an explosive of unheard-of power. No one needed to doubt that a dictator of Hitler's type would use this new means of destruction in order to achieve his aim of world domination. It seemed to the scientists absolutely imperative to produce such an explosive, if at all possible, before Germany could achieve it.

The only way to break through the stone wall of incomprehension surrounding the military establishment, which was completely absorbed by the task of

overcoming the existing state of unpreparedness in the
United States, seemed to be going directly to the President. Roosevelt understood at once. He permitted an
Advisory Committee to be called. A year after Fermi
had tried to interest the Navy, a sum of $6000 was
made available for graphite and uranium and some
silver borrowed from the Treasury for Fermi's use in
his laboratory in Chicago.

MAKING THE ATOM BOMB

Another year later the problem was still in the hands
of the Advisory Committee. Interest remained so low
that James Conant, who was responsible within the
framework of the National Defense Research Committee for these problems, proposed to drop nuclear
research until after the war.

From Europe, however, intelligence reached America concerning German work in the field of atomic explosives. These reports were later to prove greatly exaggerated. From Britain came very hopeful reports on
the feasibility of an atom bomb; so, finally, a committee of the National Academy of Sciences was appointed to report on the situation. In November 1941
a report by the chairman of this group, Arthur H.
Compton, was laid before an advisory committee at
the highest level, appointed by the President, and consisting of Vice-President Henry Wallace, Secretary of
War Henry Stimson, Vannevar Bush, James Conant
and General George Marshall. The Committee advised
the President to throw the full weight of government
support behind the project, and on December 6, 1941,
Roosevelt approved its recommendation. Within the
Army Corps of Engineers, District MANHATTAN was
created. In 1943 the project was placed entirely in the

hands of the Army, which pursued it with the single-ness of purpose dictated by its task: to end the war by the total defeat of the enemy. General Leslie R. Groves was in charge of the project from 1943 on; the highest responsibility rested with the Secretary of War.

To the gigantic project, thousands of scientists were harnessed. As long as they were convinced that an atomic race with Germany must be won in order to avoid defeat and utter destruction, there was hardly any doubt in their minds about the necessity and jus-tification of their labors. When Germany was defeated in May 1945, the race was won. Germany had not been able to produce an atomic weapon, and it was soon discovered that work on it had lagged far behind that of District MANHATTAN. The latter was approach-ing its culmination; doubts about the feasibility of the bomb no longer were warranted.

HOW TO USE THE BOMB

Whereas the scientists directly concerned with the construction of the bomb were completely absorbed by their task, those who had been more concerned with basic research leading to the anxiously awaited result began to consider the future aspects of the un-leashing of nuclear energy. Was the bomb to be used against Japan? What would be the effect of this new weapon and this new source of energy on world peace? How would the relationship with the Soviet Union, which already had begun to develop disquiet-ing aspects, be affected?

An answer to such questions had to be found. Gen-eral Groves appointed a committee under R. C. Tol-man to investigate future military uses of the bomb, possible peaceful applications of atomic energy and the use of radioactive products in medicine, science and industry. The committee's report made the Secretary of War acutely aware of the far-reaching consequences of the discovery and its technical development.

Secretary Stimson, therefore, proposed to President Truman the appointment of a committee of leading men to advise him on present and future policy in connection with the use of atomic energy. That committee, called the Interim Committee, met for the first time under the chairmanship of Stimson on May 9, 1945; it was assisted by a scientific panel. Arthur Compton relates that Stimson said in his opening remarks: "Today's prime fact is war. Our great task is to bring this war to a prompt and successful conclusion."[3]

It turned out that the Interim Committee's first task was to advise the Secretary of War on the use to be made of the bomb. There is no evidence that there was ever any serious thought of not using the new weapon once it was available. General Marshall did raise the question of whether it would not be a wiser course to keep the bomb a military secret instead of using it against Japan. Yet, this rather astonishing suggestion from the head of the Army cannot be construed as a deviation from the basic strategic principle that the enemy should be utterly defeated by the strongest possible means; Marshall's views are too well known. His proposal was based on the sound assumption that he had on hand other and absolutely secure means to defeat the Japanese—the landing of troops on the Japanese islands—whereas the bomb was not

[3] *Atomic Quest* (New York, 1956), p. 219.

yet tested and its effects most uncertain. Moreover, it was his impression that the future security of the United States would be better assured with the known weapons of war than with an unpredictable new weapon that, once it had been used, would inevitably spread to potential enemies. Events proved how right he was in this respect. Marshall did not press his view since the scientists convinced the Committee that there was no hope that atomic technology, leading to the manufacture of the bomb, would not soon be common knowledge.

The Interim Committee thereafter devoted itself to the question of how the bomb should be used to produce the unconditional surrender of Japan. There was considerable hesitation over dropping the apparatus on a target in Japan, since this would lead to indiscriminate destruction of life and property. The possibility of a demonstration over some deserted island in the Pacific in the presence of Japanese observers was considered. Yet this alternative was discarded because the Committee assumed that a mere demonstration would not be strong enough to convince the war party in Japan. Later events proved that this assumption was correct.

The proposal of the Committee, therefore, was to use the bomb as soon as possible, to use it against a military or industrial target surrounded by lighter buildings—this meant a Japanese city—and without warning. The idea of a previous warning was discarded for the good reasons that it was feared that the Japanese would move prisoners of war to the site of the announced bombing, and that the bomb finally might fail to explode.[4] General Marshall concluded

4 *Military Situation in the Far East,* pp. 561–64.

from the fact that the fire raid on Tokyo in March had not induced the Japanese Government to surrender, that only the full application of the atomic bombs could do it.

The aversion against obliteration bombing had, as we have seen, by that time completely disappeared. It had been practiced against Germany for more than two years and against Japan for two months. The fine distinction between military and non-military targets made earlier, before America was in the war, had in the meantime been lost.

What was foremost in the minds of the planners, now that they had to deal with the atom bomb, was the extraordinary nature of the weapon and its promise of precipitating Japanese surrender without a land battle, not the nature of the destruction it would cause in Japan.

SECOND THOUGHTS

As soon as the two bombs on Hiroshima and Nagasaki had brought about Japan's unconditional surrender and the war was over, the problem appeared in a different light. What had been a relatively easy decision for the President and his military advisers, whose task of ending the war with the minimum of loss was absolutely clear, became a formidable problem for the world.

First to grasp the problem in its whole extent were naturally the nuclear scientists. They had been struggling with the scientific and technological development of nuclear power for years. They were the only ones who fully knew the nature of their discovery and discerned the dim outline of its potentialities and future implications. In spite of their absorption in the war effort, they had naturally devoted much thought to the profounder meaning of their work.

In a scientific report submitted to the War Department, a committee under Professor James Franck of the University of Chicago had expressed the view that although "in the past scientists could disclaim direct responsibility for the use to which mankind had put their disinterested discoveries, we now feel compelled to take a more active stand. . . ."[5] The natural scientists, at once triumphant and shocked at their own achievements, immediately took up the investigation of the new aspects in depth. At the Metallurgical Laboratory, Chicago, at Oak Ridge and at Los Alamos associations of scientists were founded almost simultaneously. In January 1946 they founded the Federation of American Scientists. On December 15, 1945, the first issue of the *Bulletin of the Atomic Scientists* was published. It was, as Eugene Rabinowitch later put it, "a part of the conspiracy to preserve our civilization by scaring men into rationality."[6]

The scientists' concern seemed, at the outset, twofold: to avoid, at all cost, an arms race with the Soviet Union, and to drive home to the people an understanding of the colossal peril that atomic arms meant for human civilization and humanity as such.

The fear of an arms race with the Soviet Union was clearly a reflex of the physicists' own motivation in insisting on the need of developing nuclear fission into a powerful arm. They had dreaded to see these arms of a new kind and dimension in the hands of the German dictator, and had visualized their effort as an arms race with their foe. Since the relationship between the Soviet Union and her allies had begun visi-

[5] *Bulletin of the Atomic Scientists,* I, 10 (September 1946).
[6] Ibid., VII, 1 (January 1951).

bly to deteriorate even before the issue of the war, the continuation of this race seemed to them inevitable.

All the remaining opinions on the implications of the new weapons may easily be related to inherited views on strategy held and never questioned by Americans.

SCIENTISTS' AXIOMS

Since at that time the doctrine that war is to be waged with the utmost power in order to defeat the enemy was almost universally and automatically accepted, the natural scientists naturally concluded that the next war would inevitably be an atomic war. Fearing the worst, they assumed that it would be total war. From the pacifists of the nineteen twenties and thirties they had inherited the unquestioned assumption that an arms race inevitably ends in war, and that the existence of a new and overwhelming weapon will precipitate war. The experience of Pearl Harbor, which was and still is at the root of deeply held convictions, dictated to them the conclusion that a future war would necessarily begin with an atomic surprise attack.

From American idealism as expressed in the League of Nations, in the Kellogg-Briand Pact, and in the plans for the United Nations, many of the scientists had inherited the conviction that international control of nuclear energy was essential to prevent its use for destructive aims and that world government now was necessary, nay, inevitable.

The nuclear physicists were convinced that the technology that had led to the construction of the atomic bomb could not be kept secret. Its scientific basis was common knowledge, and the necessary techniques could be worked out by any industrially advanced nation willing to devote the necessary resources in talent and money to such an ambitious project. Therefore the answer had to be internationalization. Out of this conviction grew the Acheson-Lilienthal report, which was to become the Baruch Plan. That internationalization was an illusion became clear when the Soviet Union rejected it on December 1, 1946, in the United Nations—a deep shock to the natural scientists.

Large sections of the American public held quite different and naïve views. Here America wielded a new weapon which was an absolute weapon, against which there was no defense. By the mere threat of this weapon, an enemy of peace could be brought to reason. Since the Americans were and still are disposed to regard any international conflict simply as a clash between good and evil rather than as a confrontation of genuinely and perhaps legitimately opposed interests, they suddenly visualized an ultimate weapon to deter and punish the wrongdoer. And because the United States would never attack, war would henceforth be impossible.

In opposition to this optimistic tenor another pattern of public thinking developed. The second group of men and women to be immediately and deeply impressed by the transcendental nature of the new weapons and their first use in war was found, as one would expect, in the churches and among the liberal intellectuals. Led by these groups, a movement of self-accusation developed. In reaction to the ruins of Hiroshima, and human beings mortally seared by radiation, an emotion near to panic could be observed. Public opinion, once aroused by a dramatic event, is not given to calm reflection. In opposition to what a

70

superficial observer might expect and what the average American may believe, there exists in the United States an atmosphere of latent personal and collective anxiety, which, in spite of a generally courageous attitude in the face of real danger, may unleash strange reactions to imaginary dangers.[7] This creates an above average readiness for panic. In the year 1945, the self-destruction of mankind, doomsday wrought by man, seemed possible.

A sensation of panic was greatly promoted by the atomic scientists. They not only convinced many people that atomic weapons are in a class different from all other implements of war, but some scientists imparted their own feelings of guilt to as many people as possible. The most conflicting views were voiced and added to the confusion so natural at the end of a war.

Eugene Rabinowitch gives testimony to this state of affairs when he writes:

> The intrusion of scientists into public affairs undoubtedly has produced some undesirable results. It has made, in some instance, for more and not less passion and confusion, and has made some rational solutions more and not less difficult.[8]

From the whirlpool of conflicting feeling and thought, however, one common will gradually emerged. It would be intolerable to the American mind not to rationalize chaos, not to master spiritually the new forces. One major contribution came from the scientists themselves, one from the Christian churches.

[7] Urs Schwarz, "Die Angst in der Politik," *Die Angst*, Studien am C. G. Jung-Institut (Zürich, 1959), pp. 127 ff.
[8] *Bulletin of the Atomic Scientists*, VII, 1 (January 1951).

What, then, was the expression which this searching of the mind found in strategic thought? A significant change occurred. From the very small group that had devoted time and imagination to strategic thinking in earlier periods of peace and war, the urge to ask questions on the nature of war and warfare now spread to a much wider community, the world of scholarly thought and religion. The natural scientist, the sociologist, the economist, the historian, the theologian, the churchman, the philosopher became involved. Were the military men involved as well? It is difficult to find, in the period immediately following the war, convincing evidence of a new beginning. It is later, in the pages of the monumental histories of the war as prepared by the Army, the Navy, and the Air Force, and in some personal memoirs, that events are confronted with ideas.

The questions the new students of war would ask, and would be asked, in the international dialogue on the immediate past that then began, were of this kind: were the great strategic decisions of the war right? Were the chief actors not blinded by strategic shibboleths, by stereotypes, by national pride? Were political views and means not neglected in planning the defeat of the enemy? Was indiscriminate bombing necessary and can it be justified? How can disarmament be insured? How may the non-combatant be protected? What world order can avoid future wars?

On the other hand, and in opposition to this new approach to war and to thinking about war, the end of fighting had produced a formidable reaction. In the environment of spiritual exhaustion, so natural after an all-out national effort, the mind returned to traditional, ingrained patterns. The defeat of the German

72

armies on German soil, the unconditional surrender of disorganized, devastated Germany, the unconditional surrender of the Emperor of Japan brought about by the most powerful weapon ever designed and by the threat of utter destruction of his people and land, seemed to confirm in every respect the traditional concept. To the pragmatic mind the war and its issue proved that:

War is total. War has to end in total defeat of the enemy. Once war is over, nations may return to their peaceful pursuits. Civilian power will once more be paramount. There can be no other war since evil has been defeated and the peace-loving American nation is in sole possession of the ultimate weapon. If war nevertheless should recur, it will be fought with machines, not men. Long, drawn-out wars belong to the past, they will not have to be fought again.

It was this pattern of thought that shaped America in the immediate post-war period. The American forces were demobilized. Atomic energy, when the plans for internationalization proved unrealistic, was to be kept an American secret. After a dramatic fight in the House of Representatives, it was placed forever in the hands of the civilian power by the Atomic Energy Act (McMahon Act), signed by President Truman on August 1, 1946.

Disarmament was carried out most effectively in America; there was no doubt that the world would soon proceed to do likewise. No serious thought, therefore, had to be devoted to this easy problem.

JUST WAR

The liberal intellectuals in America—by no means only natural scientists, but many writers and university teachers of law, history, sociology, psychology—had generally been close to the forces advocating disarmament and had been instrumental in the peace movements. They were joined in a very effective way by the Christian churches. The churches welcomed the mood of the country at the end of the war. During the war, they had generally supported the war effort and had reconciled religious teaching with national defense, but not without earnest study and soul-searching.[9]

The Federal Council of Churches' Commission on the Relation of the Church to the War in the Light of the Christian Faith had as early as 1944 reviewed the implications of total war and of indiscriminate bombings. Before 1950 there appeared no fewer than five major reports by responsible commissions of the several Christian churches.[10] They were now concerned with a problem of new dimensions, the atomic bomb. To assess the implications of the new arms, the churches' study groups had to base their work, naturally, on the views of the assumedly most knowledgeable group, the natural scientists.

The churches as a whole accepted without further questioning the scientists' views as to the nature of future war, i.e., that it could only be total. This assumption confronted them with the need to reexamine the conceptual framework of the all-important doctrine of just war. Just war, which was waged in self-defense against armed forces, and tried as far as reasonably possible to spare non-combatants, had

[9] Robert W. Tucker, *The Just War; A Study in Contemporary American Doctrine* (Baltimore, 1960), p. 81.
[10] Robert C. Batchelder, *The Irreversible Decision, 1939–1950* (Boston, 1962), p. 238.

been reconciled with the commandments of Christ and with Christian love by generations of Christian thinkers. President Woodrow Wilson had stated the idea in moving terms, in his speech to Congress on February 26, 1917:

> My theme is of those great principles of compassion and of protection which mankind has sought to throw about human lives, the lives of non-combatants, the lives of men who are peacefully at work . . . the lives of women and children . . .

This theme of just war now seemed unrealistic because of the presumed nature of any future war. The churches tried to respond with the solution that all war should be abolished, or that war could be waged only under conditions of extreme provocation, when existence itself and the highest values, like Christianity and liberty, were at stake.

How far America had gone since the beginning of World War II may be measured by comparing the newer theories with the official pronouncements of 1939 and 1940 which, in turn, reflected to a very high degree the thinking of liberal intellectual circles. On September 1, 1939, President Roosevelt had addressed an urgent appeal to all belligerents, asking them publicly to affirm that their armed forces should, in no event and under no circumstances, undertake the bombardment from the air of civilian populations or of unfortified cities, upon the understanding that the same rules of warfare would be scrupulously observed by all their opponents. On May 1, 1940, he had proclaimed in an address to the American Red Cross: "The bombing of helpless and unprotected civilians is a tragedy which has aroused the horror of all mankind.

75

I recall with pride that the United States consistently has taken the lead in urging that this inhuman practice be prohibited."[11]

MAKING THE SUPER-BOMB

In the National Defense Research Committee and the Office of Scientific Research and Development scientists had become, as Vannevar Bush puts it, "full and responsible partners for the first time in the conduct of war."[12] However, when the government of the United States again faced a momentous strategic decision, more important perhaps than the decision of 1945 to use the atomic bomb, the influence of the scientists seemed slim. The question was whether to make the hydrogen bomb or not to make it.

As early as December 1946 John J. McCloy had publicly mentioned the possibility of a super-bomb. In the fall of 1949 Senator Edwin C. Johnson, a Democrat from Colorado, committed one of the major post-war security leaks on Capitol Hill. In a television broadcast on November 1, advocating greater secrecy in atomic matters, he disclosed that the United States had made considerable progress on a super-bomb with 1000 times the Nagasaki bomb's effectiveness. This unexpected leak caused President Truman to announce officially, on January 31, 1950, that he had "directed the Atomic Energy Commission to continue its work on all forms of atomic weapons, including the so-called super-bomb." In July of the same year—a few days after the aggression in South Korea—a request for a

[11] Samuel I. Rosenman, ed., *The Public Papers and Addresses of Franklin D. Roosevelt*, 1939 (New York, 1941), p. 454; and 1940 (New York, 1942), p. 177.
[12] *Modern Arms and Free Men* (New York, 1949), p. 6.

quarter of a billion dollars in supplementary funds for hydrogen bomb development was sent to Congress.

Vannevar Bush and James Conant—the same man who had thought in 1941 that work on nuclear energy could wait until the end of the war—were consulted by President Truman on the advisability of research into nuclear fusion and its potentialities for defense. They both advised against the development of such a weapon. Yet other advice, on which the President was to base his decision, came from the Joint Congressional Committee set up by the McMahon Act, and from the Armed Services.

The scientific community's reaction to President Truman's announcement of January 31, 1950, gives ample proof that it felt it had been completely passed over. The majority of the physicists were against the decision, which they considered strategically unsound and dangerous. They were highly critical of the "vociferous popular support" for the decision and unhappy about its congressional backing. At the assembly of the Physical Society of New York, twelve scientists signed a statement in which they urged the United States to make a solemn declaration never to use the planned new weapon first. In their statement, they inserted a clause that was in the highest degree typical of the traditional strategic thinking to be found even in such an enlightened group. They said that the only circumstances that might force the United States to use the new weapon would be if it or its allies were attacked by this same weapon.

The military and congressional leaders were duplicating the thinking process that had led some natural scientists in 1939 to draft the Einstein letter for President Roosevelt. Drawing upon their knowledge of nuclear research, and upon their knowledge of and hatred for the National Socialist government of Germany, some natural scientists had, in 1939, reached the conclusion that Germany must be prevented from using nuclear weapons. To achieve this end, a similar weapon in the hands of the United States was needed. In 1949, the members of Congress and the Chiefs of Staff had learned to assess correctly the intentions and potentialities of the Soviet rulers. The physicists had informed them that they were certain the Soviet Union was developing a hydrogen bomb and that the Russian scientists were sure to succeed. Congressional and military leaders concluded, therefore, without the consent of the scientific community, that a new arms race had become inevitable.

When in the summer of 1950 South Korea was attacked and a dangerous crisis in Europe seemed imminent, the situation appeared so serious that a spontaneous wartime reaction set in. The single-mindedness and energy which had brought the MANHATTAN District project to full success again came into play. On November 1, 1952, the first thermonuclear apparatus exploded on the island of Eniwetok, ushering in, with its flash, a new age of technology, strategy and policy.

The political and intellectual persecution of which, at that time, certain scientists who had opposed the construction of a thermonuclear bomb were the victims—most conspicuously Robert Oppenheimer, in the 1954 congressional hearings—had manifold roots in American tradition and violent American nationalism. Outbursts of this kind had occurred as far back as early colonial times, and certainly during the years of

Wilsonian enlightenment in World War I. They were, above all, a symbol of the fact that strategy was again in the hands of the military. The brief interlude when natural scientists, many of them of suspicious European origin, had lived in the illusion that "the philosophers should govern" was over.

But a contribution scientists were able to make in this period was their consistent appeal to search for means to stop the arms race. The efforts in the United Nations Disarmament Committees, which have never disappeared from the agenda of the world organization, can clearly be traced back to the *Bulletin of the Atomic Scientists*.

V

Massive Retaliation
and Limited War

MOSCOW HAS THE BOMB

In 1949 the Soviet Union exploded a nuclear device.
By copying the American bomber B-29, she acquired
a means of delivery for the few bombs she possessed.
In 1953 the Soviet Union exploded its first thermonuclear apparatus. Forcing the pace of rocketry development, Moscow could threaten, by the fall of 1956, to
annihilate European capitals with intermediate range
ballistic missiles. In August 1957 successful rocket tests
and in October of the same year the spectacular success of "Sputnik" disclosed that the Soviet Union had
or at least might have intercontinental ballistic missiles.

The United States during this period was covered
by the majestic display of the heavy bombers of the
Strategic Air Command on airfields in continental
America and of medium bombers on a far-flung range
of advanced bases in allied countries. The preference
of the strategic planners had originally been the
bomber rather than the missile, a decision explained
by their belief that in strategic warfare they would
have to rely on the thermonuclear bomb, which was
thought too heavy for delivery by the missiles then
being contemplated as reasonably feasible in America.

The experience of the war had added to the

strength of the argument for the bomber. A bomber had carried the first atomic weapons to Japan. Bombers had contributed greatly to the destruction of the German war machine, and had helped to make Japan ready for unconditional surrender. The bomber was the successor of the battleship, whose role had been to defeat the enemy fleet in faraway seas. The missiles that the Germans had deployed in the last period of the war had, on the contrary, proved ineffective in destroying the morale and the industrial capacity of Britain. These were hard facts, and it needed much imagination to give second thoughts to the conclusion that the pragmatist could so easily draw from them. No one could predict the accuracy of the missiles developed later. The bomber was rightly considered far more accurate. To this was added the almost irrational attachment of the Air Force to bombers, which exists even today.

It is true that the Department of Defense had set up a study right after the war on the possibility of developing long-range missiles for atomic warheads with German experts, but this project was canceled as early as 1947. It was reactivated by the Air Force in 1951, and studies by The RAND Corporation in the weapons and missile field led to the 1954 decision to develop the Atlas ICBM.

As early as 1946 the Air Force had signed several research contracts in the field of long-range missiles. Only two types, however, reached a developed stage, namely the air-breathing "Snark" and "Navaho" and a ballistic missile "Atlas." Progress was slow until 1952.

In August 1952, a conference of senior officers of the three services, of representatives of the Atomic Energy Commission and of leading industrial firms was called in order to discuss the reports of two hundred German

81

experts just returned from the Soviet Union where they had co-operated in rocketry projects. Most of them had worked on the German projects at Peene-münde, and later, while they were prisoners of war, had put their experience in the service of the Soviets. They asserted that by 1958 the Soviet Union would be able to send a re-entry vehicle weighing about four tons to any part of the United States. Now things began to move.

Early in 1953 Trevor Gardner, an engineer who had immigrated from England, was appointed special assistant for research and development to Air Force Secretary Harold E. Talbott. He at once proposed a Missile Evaluation Committee under John von Neumann, which initiated its studies in November 1953 and submitted its report the following March. It suggested that full priority be given to the development of ballistic missiles and that the problem could be solved within five to six years. At the same time The RAND Corporation submitted to the Air Force a report on the subject, which reached similar conclusions.

The year 1957 brought full recognition of the need for an intercontinental missile force capable of complementing the bomber force. Thanks to the studies of The RAND Corporation, undertaken in 1954 and conducted by A. Wohlstetter, the vulnerability of the bomber force in its then existing deployment had been fully recognized. Great improvements in its protection against surprise attack had been introduced. But complete reliance on the traditional means of delivery of the strategic weapons would no longer suffice in the face of rapidly developing missile technology.

It had needed Pearl Harbor to persuade a complacent public opinion to consent to an all-out war effort. Without Pearl Harbor the Japanese would probably have been allowed to make wide inroads in Southeast Asia without American interference, and to consolidate their grip on their vast new empire. In the same way that the sneak attack of 1941 turned out to be a major strategic blunder on the part of the Japanese, the "Sputnik" of 1957 was one of the strategic blunders of Chairman Khrushchev. Only his combination of a threat to the security of the United States with a demonstration of superior scientific achievement and technological skill could shake the well-satisfied American public of the Eisenhower years. This was a direct challenge. A backward country had overtaken America, the leader in the field of science, invention, industrial production and efficiency—America, thought to be so permanently and inherently superior to the rest of the world. Soul-searching, self-accusation, and wild determination were the result. Without the humiliating presence of the first artificial satellite launched by the Soviet Union, it is likely that the decision of 1954 to proceed with the Atlas ICBM program would not have been implemented until a much later date.

While these technological and moral developments were taking place, the United States Government developed and confirmed the strategic doctrine of massive retaliation. In his speech of January 12, 1954, before the Council on Foreign Relations in New York, the Secretary of State, John Foster Dulles, made the now classic statement of the administration's strategic thinking.[1] This military program had been developed much earlier, before the inauguration of President Eisenhower, when the future Secretary of State, in

[1] U. S. *Department of State Bulletin*, XXX (January 25, 1954), 107–10.

conjunction with Admiral Radford, had drawn up plans for the future conduct of foreign policy.

MASSIVE RETALIATION AND SECOND THOUGHTS

In an address that was widely commented on, Admiral Radford, the Chairman of the Joint Chiefs of Staff, speaking in Washington on December 14, 1953, had stressed the aspects of the new military policy, which was by then termed the New Look. He underlined that it would be impossible to sustain combat-effective units of superior strength in every place where aggression might occur, and proclaimed the determination to maintain national airpower superior to that of any other nation in the world.[2]

The New Look concept of Eisenhower's first administration which by 1953 had already been rendered obsolete by events and by private strategic study, must not be judged too harshly. It was very much the Old Look, which had prevailed unquestioned throughout the period between the two World Wars and during the Second World War, and which still dominated the opinion of an uninformed public as well as of badly informed leaders. In the election campaign of 1952 the promise to end the war in Korea had been a powerful Republican argument. The country was distressed by the fact that its youth was again fighting a bloody war in the mountains and rice fields of a faraway Asian country. America's technical superiority, its power and might, the bomb, seemed of no avail against a cunning foe who did not count human lives. This war had to be finished soon, and such a war should never, never occur again. And it is only just to

[2] *Documents on American Foreign Relations, 1953* (New York, 1953), p. 64.

remember that similar views were held and expressed in the United Kingdom. This was the emotional state of the country, and both Eisenhower and Dulles, determined to follow the mood of the electorate and to march behind their troops, could not think of strategy in terms other than those that would correspond to popular feeling.

However, one side of the argument was impressive. It started from the assumption that there were two threats to national security, one military, one economic. A proper balance between a strong economy and strong military forces, therefore, was necessary. Where the Eisenhower administration failed was in its assessment of what weight the United States economy could carry.

In his address of January 12, 1954, John Foster Dulles started with a remarkable critical assessment of the tendency of American foreign policy and strategy, that of always waiting for the enemy's moves and of merely reacting to them. But he offered no solution and withdrew instead behind a new line of defense, the advantage of which would be its cheapness. He saw the solution for a national strategy in placing more reliance on deterrent power and less on local defensive power. Deterrence seemed to him the modern way of getting maximum protection at a supportable cost. Local defense would, as he put it, always be important, but it had to be reinforced by the further deterrent of massive retaliatory power.

The doctrine was further interpreted, both by Mr. Dulles and by other speakers for the Administration, as meaning that massive retaliation was to be used not only against local wrongdoers and aggressors, but also against the sources of aggressiveness, such as the Soviet Union and Communist China.

Within a few months this conception had suffered a significant defeat. France had lost the war in Indochina, and it had not been possible to come to her help with a massive or a local atomic intervention. To the American leaders such a step, after careful consideration, seemed out of proportion to the interests at stake. And the international environment was definitely against it. The European Defense Community had failed, and it was on the Community's strength that the Administration had hoped to build its European defense without on-the-spot American forces. The New Look strategy had come under fire in the United States as well as in the allied countries.

On November 29, 1954, therefore, in an address in Chicago Mr. Dulles slightly refurbished his and Admiral Radford's doctrine when he said:

> Now you may ask does this mean that any local war would automatically be turned into a general war with atomic bombs being dropped all over the map? The answer is no. The essential thing is that we and our allies should have the means and the will to assure that a potential aggressor would lose from his aggression more than he could gain. This does not mean that the aggressor has to be totally destroyed. It does mean a capacity to inflict punishing damage.[3]

In total opposition to such strategic thinking a body of thought had been developing for several years in intellectual circles, which, after their participation in the war effort, no longer felt unconcerned with military strategy. It was essentially the development in East Asia, to which America traditionally is extremely

[3] *Documents on American Foreign Relations, 1954* (New York, 1954), p. 18.

sensitive, that shattered the reliance on absolute weapons. In spite of massive economic assistance and help in the form of munitions and friendly advice, in spite of a generous attempt at mediation between Nationalists and Communists entrusted to General Marshall in the years 1945 to 1947, China had, by September 1949, fallen into the hands of the Communists. America had "lost China," as the event was popularly described. The atomic bomb seemed meaningless in the face of these developments.

A group of professors of the Massachusetts Institute of Technology and of Harvard University started discussion of this complex of problems as early as 1949 in a private circle. Their findings, drawing attention to the danger of too exclusive a reliance on strategic nuclear deterrence, were significant at such an early date, and even more so because several members of the group, such as McGeorge Bundy, Carl Kaysen, Jerome B. Wiesner, Arthur M. Schlesinger, in later years became directly involved in shaping official doctrine.

In the summer of 1950 Communist forces from North Korea crossed the 38th parallel and invaded the Republic of South Korea. The U. S. Air Force and Navy, which were immediately ready to come to the rescue of the Republic of South Korea, discovered within a few days that they could not bring to bear their full weight in the hills and mountains of an Asian peninsula. American conventional forces were needed. They were hastily thrown piecemeal into the battle. But they could not stem the flood; they had to reconquer the lost ground step by step. Naval superiority in the area, the most massive air force in existence, and the atomic bomb, which could not be used, had proved powerless.

The event had a deep impact on strategic thinking in America. One may assert that nothing else has ever changed the course of a nation's thinking in the special field of military strategy more than the outbreak of this war. The making of the atomic bomb, the explosion of it in the war, had brought a new category of planners into the field and had opened new ways of thinking. Yet it had not really modified basic concepts held for a century, but rather had confirmed them. Now the outbreak of a new limited war on the ground, the kind of war that would never, never happen again, opened the way to a fully new approach.

The most significant sign of this breakthrough is found in the words of Eugene Rabinowitch in the *Bulletin of the Atomic Scientists* of July 1950:

> If we concentrate on fabrication of weapons of mass destruction, and do not balance this development by the creation of sufficiently large, well-supplied, and strategically distributed land forces, we will run a double danger: We will be in danger of losing out in peripheral skirmishes with Soviet satellites, such as the Korean war; and we will have deprived ourselves of freedom of decision in the event of an open Soviet aggression against nations of the Atlantic Pact. If we have nothing but atomic bombs with which to strike back, we will obviously be forced to use these weapons—even if the enemy does not do so first, and even if our leaders have grave doubts about the political wisdom and moral justification of their use.[4]

Thus the theme for new thinking and a new approach was set. It took ten years before the new ideas were fully translated into defense policy. These years produced an enormous body of writings—some of them classified at the outset and later divulged, some of

[4] Op. cit., VI, 7 (July 1950), 217.

them from the beginning addressed to the thinking public, some to the unthinking public.

The changing pattern of thought was conditioned by four main elements: The first was each writer's personal point of view and the question of whether he had been more exposed to traditional military thinking or to the scientist's approach. The second element was changing technology, which several times altered the objective basis of reflection. The third element of change was the development in the Communist world and in Communist strategy, since the whole debate evolved within the assumption that defense was concerned only with defense against the Communist threat. The fourth element of change can be found in developing theory itself, in which new results naturally condition the subsequent steps.

Doubts about the validity of deterrence by means of the threat of massive retaliation originated simultaneously wherever imaginative thinkers confronted the theory of the New Look with existing or possible politico-military scenarios. They soon discovered that threats lacked credibility. It was along this line that the most significant criticism of the official doctrine developed.

It would be an oversimplification if we were to distinguish between a traditionalist approach and a progressive approach, and attribute one to government and official military thinking and the other to private thinkers, authors or institutes. We will find traditionalism in the widest sense in private thinking and a very early intrusion of scientific thinking of the highest caliber into the field of official planning. Yet basically, the Eisenhower administration, fettered by political promises, tended rather to rationalize away the facts of modern technology and of a completely changed political environment when they did not correspond to the economic doctrine of a balanced budget and, in a lesser degree, to the views and opinions gathered during World War II. The scientific community, on the other hand, was better prepared by its whole outlook toward research and discovery to approach new situations with open minds and with as few preconceived ideas as possible.

Looking back over the years in which the strategy of massive retaliation grew and vanished, one has to admit that, historically speaking, in spite of its failures in certain areas, it was not altogether ineffective. When Mr. Dulles announced the strategy, he was reflecting the changes that had taken place since the outbreak of the Korean War. In 1950 the United States still practically held the nuclear monopoly. In 1954 the monopoly was lost, but the United States had acquired the capability of massive and prompt retaliation. Therefore a repetition in some other place of the type of attack made against South Korea in 1950 had become more dangerous for the Soviet Union. The fact is that no other open aggression has occurred since. In this sense the threat of massive retaliation seems to have been effective.

The threat of total strategic war, which the doctrine of massive retaliation held out, had, as the American Sovietologist Herbert S. Dinerstein points out, a deep influence on Soviet ideology. The idea that war was the most effective means for fostering the Communist Revolution gradually vanished from Soviet textbooks. Nuclear war was too destructive and its results could be fatal for both the Socialist and the Capitalist camps.

Since the Chinese Communists did not share this view of modern strategy, the difference in interpretation greatly widened the ideological split, which had been growing for a long time and for varied reasons. So we may assert that the doctrine of massive retaliation has been an instrument for the disruption in the Communist camp.

SHIELD AND SWORD

One of the most significant illustrations of American strategic thought at the highest official level in the mid-fifties is President Eisenhower's letter of January 5, 1955, to Secretary of Defense Wilson.[5] The letter was the product of thorough study by the President's civilian and military advisers. The personal views of the President and of his Secretary of State are also clearly visible in the document.

The President departs completely from the view traditionally held by the American public that American security is threatened only at particular times and by particular enemies, and states flatly that the threat is continuing and many-sided. It demands, therefore, a constant exertion, a systematic build-up of security forces in the widest sense, within the limits of the capabilities of the national economy. The letter insists on the role of science and technology, of which maximum use is to be made in order to minimize the need for numbers in men. The President admits that for the first time in history America is exposed to sudden attack. Having expressed these thoughts, which embody the immediate heritage of World War II, the letter reverts to more traditional views, which do not yet seem to be aware of the basic facts of the missile age.

The long-range program of military requirements is based on the assumption that if hostilities should break

[5] *U. S. Department of State Bulletin*, XXXII (January 17, 1955), 87 f.

out, the United States would be able to use its industrial capabilities, as always, in order to build up the forces that would finally defeat the enemy. Strong retaliatory power is to be maintained to achieve a twofold effect: to prevent the outbreak of a major war and, if deterrence fails, to punish an aggressor. Continental aerial defense is recognized as an integral part of retaliatory capability. In case of actual major war, navies and armies are to play, after the nuclear exchange, their traditional World War II roles.

Limited war, in the form of local war, is plainly visualized in the Eisenhower document, which acknowledges that conventional forces are necessary for this kind of conflict. But according to the views of John F. Dulles and Admiral Radford, in case of such a war growing reliance should be placed on the forces of allied nations, whose availability and capabilities were at that time viewed with surprising optimism. The United States would support these allied troops with a central reserve of mobile forces, envisioned as rather small in size since, owing to the lack of adequate air transport, such a force could not be brought to a theater of operations in large numbers. Interestingly enough, no mention is made and no thought is given to what we customarily term sub-limited war, war by infiltration and subversion.

This document presented a much more modern and flexible strategy than earlier statements of the Eisenhower administration, with their accent on massive retaliation. It encouraged General Maxwell D. Taylor, Army Chief of Staff, to submit to the Joint Chiefs of Staff early in 1956 a document entitled "A National Military Program" which for the first time opposed to the concept of massive retaliation in full the concept of the strategy of flexible response. It was defeated in the continued fights between the heads of the Armed Services, which were more bitter during the Eisenhower period than at any other time.

Admiral Radford, the Chairman of the Joint Chiefs of Staff, in turn introduced in July 1956 a plan that called for an almost complete return to the original concept of massive retaliation. When the contents of this document became known to the world through the so-called Radford leak, it had the most devastating effect upon the allies of the United States. Historically speaking, it was to become the source of most of the conflicts and misunderstandings that ever since have bedevilled the alliances of the West. It presented to the eye of the innocent foreign observer and to allied governments the image of a "Fortress America" which would protect itself and its allies by the threat of strategic retaliation in case general war occurred. General war was a conflict in which the Soviet Union and the United States would be directly involved and in which nuclear weapons would be used at the outset. For local wars the United States would initially rely on the allies, giving them what little help it could until its great potential in industry and manpower could as usual be brought into play at a later date for their liberation.

This pattern of thought, quite naturally, was generally reflected in the strategic doctrine applied to the North Atlantic Treaty Organization. NATO's limited ground forces—the German *Bundeswehr* was at that time only a project—would serve as a "shield" protecting the boundaries of the allied countries. To strengthen this shield, nuclear weapons were assigned to the Tactical Air Forces. Some artillery and missile units with nuclear capability reinforced operationally important sectors. It was recognized that the shield would not be strong enough to stop or repel a massive attack against Western Europe. Yet it was anticipated that it would force the Soviet Union to deploy its full strength and thereby disclose its aggressive intention; whereupon the "sword," massive retaliation by the Strategic Air Command, would descend.

The shield was, at this early stage, described with undeniable realism as a mere "trip wire," which does not in itself stop an intruder, but tips off a destructive explosion. Since words are hard to kill, the "trip-wire" notion, as well as the words "shield and sword" in their original meaning, survived for many years, long after the strategic doctrine was dead. They may be alive, even now, in some remote corners of the minds of European and American news commentators, political leaders and government officials.

THE CONCEPT OF LIMITED WAR

The outbreak of the Korean War had initiated deep research and study within the Armed Services on the adequacy, in a visibly changing environment, of their equipment, methods and strategic concepts inherited mainly from the last period of World War II. In the ensuing debate, which reached a climax every year in the allocation of budgetary provisions to the four Armed Services, the Army, Navy and Marines generally lined up against the Air Force. It cannot be overlooked that these conflicts about money allocations produced, at the same time, a great wealth of strategic thought. This development of strategic thinking and its results, which still are the most influential factors in the determination of actual military policy, has been brilliantly narrated by General Maxwell D. Taylor in his book *The Uncertain Trumpet*.[6]

[6] New York, 1959.

What, in the meantime, had been achieved by the community of strategic thinkers and the institutions devoted to scientific research in the field of military strategy? After the challenging article published in the *Bulletin of the Atomic Scientists* shortly after the outbreak of the Korean War (see above, p. 88), the papers produced by political science institutions multiplied and began to overflow into scientific and more popular publications. In their unclassified contributions to the periodical press, the authors of classified studies, especially those on the staff of The RAND Corporation, gradually familiarized the public with sophisticated thinking on the emerging strategic problems.

The term "limited war" was conspicuously used for the first time by General George Marshall in May of 1951. In the hearings before the Senate Committees on the Armed Services and on Foreign Relations concerning the military situation in the Far East, the Secretary of Defense was asked by Senator Cain how he would characterize the conflict in Korea. Would he call it a police action or a war, and if it was a war, would he define it as a large or a small war? General Marshall replied: "I would characterize it as a limited war which I hope will remain limited."[7]

A specialized bibliography on limited war, published in 1962 by the Harvard University Center for International Affairs, lists no fewer than 328 entries.[8] While it is impossible to assess the relative importance of each contribution, and to single out one of them as the initial impulse in the chain reaction which was to

[7] *Military Situation in the Far East,* p. 610.
[8] Morton H. Halperin, *Limited War; An Essay on the Development of the Theory and an Annotated Bibliography* (Cambridge, Mass., 1962).

revolutionize American strategic thinking, it is possible to point to articles and books that were particularly instrumental in making the new problems generally known. Among these were Bernard Brodie's article, "Unlimited Weapons and Limited War,"[9] and Henry Kissinger's "Military Policy and Defense of the 'Grey Areas.'"[10] One of the earliest depth analyses was produced at the Princeton Center for International Studies in 1954 under the direction of William W. Kaufmann in the memorandum, *The Requirements of Deterrence*.[11]

It lists requirements of deterrence in the following order: capability, i.e., the existence of the necessary weapons and means of delivery; a degree of damage to the enemy that would make aggression too costly; intention, i.e., strength of will to run the risk involved in using the deterrent. In this context, capability of a power to conduct, if necessary, a limited war, became more and more the prerequisite of the complete and credible deterrent.

The suggestions of measures to increase credibility had both military and political dimensions. The military measures were intended to add to the strategic deterrent capabilities sufficient conventional strength to be deployed in danger areas as well as in the form of a strategic reserve, so that adequate means would exist to deter minor aggressions without recourse to central nuclear war. A further step in this direction was to be the build-up of continental defenses. Political measures were to consist of the building of alli-

[9] *The Reporter*, XI, 9 (November 1954), 16–21.
[10] *Foreign Affairs*, XXXIII (April 1955), 416–28.
[11] This memorandum (no. 7) was later published in the book, *Military Policy and National Security*, William W. Kaufmann, ed. (Princeton, 1956).

ances and their skillful use as threat or promise, or even direct promises of concessions in given circumstances and in exchange for valuable concessions or guarantees. In later developments, the political elements gradually receded into the background, while the military components of a credible deterrence and their combination and application came to the forefront.

As early as 1956 Arnold Wolfers devoted a study to the specific question of whether war in Europe would necessarily be unlimited nuclear war. He reached the conclusion that this escalation could be avoided.[12] His argument was that obliteration bombing would probably not be in the interest of either side and would, therefore, be mutually avoided. Rear Admiral Sir Anthony Buzzard made, at the same time, a similar contribution from the British side.[13]

Most of these studies started from recognition of the existing factors: for example, the threats to Berlin, the Korean War and the war in Indochina. Foreign policy could no longer be conducted with only two instruments—weak and timid allies and a strategic air power of overwhelming might, which, when used, would involve the United States in a general war, bringing utter destruction to her and to the countries she intended to protect, and producing far-reaching consequences in the whole world, impossible to assess in kind or extent. Scholars went on to define what limitation of warfare meant and by what methods a war might be limited, and many elements of thinking novel for America were introduced.

[12] "Could a War in Europe Be Limited?" *Yale Review*, XLV (1956).
[13] "Massive Retaliation and Graduated Deterrence," *World Politics*, VIII, 2 (January 1956).

In order to limit war it was proposed to limit its objectives. Instead of total victory, unconditional surrender of the enemy and other familiar concepts of the total war strategy of the Civil War/World War II type, a new conceptual framework was visualized. War aims and objectives might now range from resumption of negotiations, under imposed conditions advantageous to an ally or to the United States, to over-all settlements in the domain of world organization or arms control. Other methods considered were the limiting of the forces applied. In the words of William W. Kaufmann, "We are flung into a strait jacket of rationality which prevents us from lashing out at the enemy."[14] Out of this new type of thinking arose the lively debate as to the use or non-use of nuclear weapons, or eventually their limited use.

THE CONCEPT OF DETERRENCE

Since strategic power with the capability of mass destruction may be used as a deterrent of war, the possibility of using it for limiting war is a logical concomitant, which leads in turn to research into the possibility of limiting war by the threat of total war. Another question now asked was whether the balance of strategic power would allow such a use of the deterrent for limiting war, and what the relationship of limited war to the strategic balance in those circumstances would be.

When, in October 1957, the Soviet Union put the first artificial satellite into orbit, one of the effects on America was a sudden increase in interest in a scholarly approach to national problems of war and peace.

[14] *Military Policy and National Security* (Princeton, 1956), p. 129.

Writings that up to then had attracted only mild interest from a small segment of the public and had been ignored by many of the most responsible policymakers suddenly gained a wide appeal. An explosion of public interest carried them to the surface, with the result that a work like Harvard Professor Henry A. Kissinger's *Nuclear Weapons and Foreign Policy*[15] was read and discussed not only by officials and civic leaders, but by a much broader public. The great achievement of the book was that it definitely linked strategy with the political aims to which the nation was committed. It introduced the Clausewitz concept of war in its correctly understood and interpreted application to American thought, and was probably the most effective contribution to the destruction of old shibboleths and preconceptions in this field. Almost simultaneously the book *Limited War* by Robert E. Osgood[16] appeared and added new perspectives to the discussion.

Testimony of the sudden interest in the question of strategic policies was the report submitted in 1957 to the Administration by a group headed by H. Rowan Gaither. Never published and still kept secret, it described the relative strength of the United States and the Soviet Union and drew conclusions that inspired serious concern. The Rockefeller Brothers Fund published, on January 5, 1958, a similar report, in which the danger of the United States falling behind in military technology was denounced and an improvement of its posture both for all-out and limited war was demanded.[17]

[15] New York, 1957.
[16] Chicago, 1957.
[17] *The United States in World Affairs, 1958–1959,* I (New York, 1959), pp. 103 f.

The strategic thesis of the important Kissinger book was, in a nutshell, that the most effective deterrent to substantial aggression is the knowledge that the United States would from the very outset employ small nuclear weapons on the battlefield. The evolution of the author's thinking can be seen in his next book, *The Necessity for Choice*.[18] At the same time the book reflects the development of strategic thought in the armed forces and in the scientific community. Kissinger now stresses the equal necessity for evolving a politico-military environment for strong conventional armaments—the importance of which he had never denied. Ideally conventional armaments should be so strong that they could be overcome only by the nuclear weapons of an aggressor. Nuclear defense thus would become the last, but not the only recourse. It is evident that the full panoply of nuclear arms has to be available to sustain such a strategy. Such strength would, in Kissinger's view, increase the flexibility of diplomacy and make possible reasonable negotiations about the control of nuclear weapons.

Parallel with these studies directed at making deterrence effective and limiting a war in case deterrence failed, and as their logical outcome, scientific research into the potentials of arms control and disarmament for furthering these same strategic aims unfolded.

The searching discussion of modern arms as instruments of international and national policy had now come full circle:

First, it started from the terrifying fact that with nuclear fission and nuclear fusion a wealth of arms had been created, which, because of their universally

18 New York, 1961.

devastating and politically unpredictable effects, were too dangerous to be wielded by mortal beings (1946). Such arms had to be abolished or rendered sterile by being entrusted to a world government.

Second, when the Soviet Union had acquired similar weapons, a balance of terror was found to exist between the two world super-powers (1954). Theory began to concentrate on the evaluation of this balance, its elements, its stability and its effects on world politics.

Third, the apparent stability of mutual deterrence, making the use of strategic nuclear weapons unlikely or impossible, promoted the study of the concept of limited war (1956). In the course of these evaluations the fact clearly emerged—it was as old as mankind and as old as war—that armaments for limited war, whether conventional or nuclear, also play the role of a deterrent to aggression.

Fourth, it had to be recognized that deterrence was not the province of strategic nuclear weapons alone, nor of conventional force alone, but had to be discussed as a particular effect of any given weapons system. The center of future research, strategic planning and evaluation, had to be deterrence as such (1960).

Fifth, it had now become fully clear, owing to the work of American scholars, that in addition to weapons systems, other elements not of a military dimension were necessary for deterrence in the broader modern sense. Diplomacy, signals given to the other side, proposals for arms control, statements of policy, doing or not-doing, disclosure of secrets to the other side and penetration into the secrets of the potential enemy had to be understood as being quite as important as weapons (1962). Weapons could, in fact, be considered as deterrent only in the context of a much

101

wider set of measures which, taken together, amount to a strategy.

In the special context of American strategic thought, the discovery of deterrence as an object of combined strategy acquires added significance. Whereas for European states, large and small, and for any tribe in the Naga Hills or the Central African Bush, it was and is an axiom of security to deter a potential aggressor by some kind of display of power, the United States hardly needed this concept. The insular situation and the peaceful and just demeanor of its government seemed sufficient to make an attack unlikely. To use military power for political ends, to impress the outside world, seemed altogether immoral. Should war unhappily occur, the enemy would be dealt with by the forces that might be considered adequate and mobilized for the occasion.

The introduction of deterrence into the political and military vocabulary is, therefore, for America, an innovation. The deep understanding of its meaning and mechanism acquired by systematic research, and its description in the newest literature, is—in spite of the inevitable aberrations, confusions and gaps—an important American contribution and a service to the world.

THE CONCEPT OF TERROR

An additional result of this fusion of all elements of power into one system designed to deter aggression and insure peace was a new evaluation of the nature of nuclear weapons. The deep, fundamental distinction between conventional and nuclear weapons had to be revised. This distinction had been thrust on the world when the first atomic bomb exploded over Hiroshima. Since the end of the war was to be accelerated by the atomic bomb's effect on morale, it was in the highest interest of its inventors to stress as forcefully as possible that this was a terrible weapon, new and different in kind.

The terroristic aspect of the weapon had been, as we have seen, foremost in the minds of its creators throughout the years that they worked to achieve it. They expected in 1941 that Germany would develop such a bomb and use it in a ruthless, mad, and terroristic way. Therefore the United States had to construct it first in order to discourage such use.

The military men, on the other hand, were hardly touched by this aspect of the problem. They thought of the atomic bomb as a bigger and better bomb, and certainly intended to use it as if it were any other powerful weapon when they saw a need for it in the context of their operations.

But the public was deeply, and almost exclusively, impressed by the extreme terror the "hellish weapon" inspired. Pacifist propaganda has never stopped stressing this aspect and this aspect alone, exploiting it for its own purposes. Communist propaganda, after trying to ignore the bomb for several years, finally turned to using the most sinister aspects of nuclear weaponry for political pressure and blackmail. In an early phase painting the horrible effects of the opponent's arms was to discourage him; in a second phase the terror wrought by the Soviet Union's thermonuclear armament was employed to the same effect.

The new concept of deterrence, or rather the return to the age-old meaning of the term, according to which all elements of national power must contribute to discourage aggression, suggests that the artificially created but simple contrast between conventional and nuclear weapons systems will in time yield to more

103

sophisticated differentiation. In its present over-simplified form the distinction creates endless problems for both the strategic planner and the advocate of disarmament, problems that are almost impossible to solve because of the emotional and illogical description of the situation. So long as in the minds of military men, of governments, of strategic thinkers and of the public at large the whole range of weapons that now confront our modern world—nuclear and non-nuclear—is not understood as the military environment within which we have to live or to die, or from which we may, at some time, be able to free ourselves, the way to nationally designed measures of arms control seems barred.

VI

Thinking About the Unthinkable

NEW METHODS

The need to use precise scientific methods to solve complicated technological problems and prepare involved military operations was strongly felt in Great Britain at the very beginning of World War II. Difficult problems of sea transportation, of submarine war, of the bomber offensive against Germany could no more be solved by simple rule of thumb and with the help of experience and plain common sense. Experience and common sense had, in many instances, inspired the wrong decision.

Similar methods had to be applied, in the United States, to solve the tremendous problems involved in making the atom bomb. One of the scientists who contributed greatly toward this work was the eminent Hungarian mathematician John von Neumann. Neumann had come in 1930 to Princeton University and moved in 1933 to the Institute for Advanced Studies. In 1928 he had published his *Theorie der Gesellschaftsspiele* and used it for analyzing the behavior of persons in their economic dealings. His theories could readily be applied to the intercourse between opponents in war. The mathematical theory of games, as developed by Neumann and Oskar Morgenstern in their joint publication *Theory of Games and Economic*

Behaviour[1] proved to be extremely challenging. Literature on the subject grew in a short time to several hundred books, all concerned with the theory of decision both in economic life and in warfare. The book also provided much of the terminology that was later applied to the discussion of strategic problems.

As Klaus Knorr, an economist and the director of Princeton University's Center for International Studies, wrote in a foreword to Herman Kahn's book *On Thermonuclear War*, "the problems of defense have become inordinately complex, and their solution is not susceptible to the rules of thumb, often called principles, which the military derived from past experience."[2] It was felt that without the use and comparison of definite figures, of quantitative analysis (which does not necessarily mean that problems are to be clothed in mathematical forms), many strategic questions could no longer be reliably answered.

The fact that many of the new semi-private research institutes and universities concerned with strategic thinking are using methods like operations research, systems analysis, and mathematical theory of games and are even reverting to the services of computers or the staging of war games has given rise to the notion that strategic theory in America is based on technological gadgetry. Nothing could be less correct. The methods of strategic analysis used today by both military and civilian institutions are based on the assumption that all problems of security have to be examined as objectively and completely as possible and that every approach that is felt to be useful may be employed.

Strategic decisions remain, in spite of the important

1 Princeton, 1943.
2 Princeton, 1960, p. v.

services of strategic expertise of this kind, the province of the decision-maker, the appointed and responsible leader.

ANALYSIS OF TOTAL WAR

It was only reluctantly that the analysts began to approach the frightening problems involved in the possibility of thermonuclear war. Yet, since the weapons systems for this type of war are kept in readiness, and are steadily expanded and improved, the need to come to grips with their full strategic meaning became urgent. Because this type of war was generally accepted as being a part of deterrence, which in turn was accepted as being the very object of national strategy, it had to be analyzed in depth.

As in other phases of the recent development of strategic theory, we find a preliminary first stage of "subterranean" research, classified studies and expert discussions, which then suddenly break out into the open through the agency of a leading statement. Even this second stage of development generally comes to the cognizance of a relatively limited group. Only much later a third phase may follow, where a wider public begins to understand the implications. A fourth stage will be reached when the outside world, especially Europe, takes notice and tries to comprehend the meaning of the new body of thought and to apply it to its own thinking on security and the future. So far as this phase of the subject is concerned, considering the present rate of growth of informed public opinion and of research in Europe, stages three and four can come only very late.

The opening statement of the new phase of wrestling with the strategy of thermonuclear war was a short article by Albert Wohlstetter, a member of The RAND Corporation, published at the beginning of 1959.[3] The theme of this article, "The Delicate Balance of Terror," was to prove that there is no such thing as an atomic stalemate, and that the strategic balance does not automatically exclude central nuclear war. The balance can be stabilized, but only at the cost of constant and intelligent effort.

Fundamental for all the work which was to follow was the book *Strategy in the Missile Age* by Bernard Brodie, a study undertaken by The RAND Corporation as part of its research for the U. S. Air Force, completed in March 1959.[4] The author of this remarkable book may be considered the first writer on strategy of the contemporary generation since his *Sea Power in the Machine Age* was published in 1941.[5] In the 1959 study there unfolded the whole method and vocabulary of strategic thinking that was to mark the transition from the fifties to the sixties.

Employing the wealth of experience assembled at The RAND Corporation, and its techniques of establishing cross sections of all available thought, Brodie not only linked the then prevailing situation with past strategic doctrines and historic experience, but brushed in a striking picture of possible future developments. He drew the attention of his readers to the fact that deterrence has no meaning unless one is fully prepared to fight a war if deterrence fails. He proposed a consistent body of strategies which might be employed, ranging from continental defense, civil defense and protection of strategic air power to limited war.

[3] *Foreign Affairs*, XXXVII, 2 (January 1959), 211–34.
[4] Princeton, 1959.
[5] Princeton, 1941.

These ideas, with special emphasis on the possibility of central thermonuclear war and its implications, were expanded and promoted in an especially powerful way by another member of RAND, the physicist and economist Herman Kahn. In a series of lectures given in March 1959 at the Center for International Studies at Princeton University, and repeated in many places, Kahn exposed a wide range of the scientific community as well as the higher levels of command of the Armed Services to this type of new thought. The lectures were published in the volume *On Thermonuclear War*.[6]

This book was followed two years later by another study by Kahn, *Thinking About the Unthinkable*, which greatly expanded and illuminated the theme. It had a preface by the French writer Raymond Aron, and its title has inspired the title of the present chapter of this book.[7]

The work of Brodie, Wohlstetter and Kahn has all grown, as we have seen, from studies undertaken at The RAND Corporation in Santa Monica, California, to which they once belonged or still belong. This organization grew out of the Air Force Project RAND, set up in May 1946 as an independent division of the Douglas Aircraft Company, in order to ensure the continuation of the kind of scientific advice upon which the Air Force had drawn during the war. It was transformed in November 1948 into an independent nonprofit organization. It is a unique establishment that attracts scholars in the fields of both natural and political sciences, in order to encourage independent study that might be important for the security of the United States. It includes such departments as Eco-

[6] Princeton, 1960.
[7] New York, 1962.

nomics, Social Sciences, Systems Operation, Physics and Mathematics.

On Thermonuclear War met with wide approval, but with some sharp criticism as well. As the author himself explains, this criticism was—significantly—often concerned mainly with whether such a book should have been written at all. Kahn said:

> It is characteristic of our times that many intelligent and sincere people are willing to argue that it is immoral to think and even more immoral to write in detail about having to fight a thermonuclear war. By and large this criticism was not personal; it simply reflected the fact that we Americans and many people throughout the world are not prepared to face reality, that we transfer our horror of thermonuclear war to reports about the realities of thermonuclear war.[8]

We may add that not only the unwillingness to think about this particularly atrocious form of war may have led to criticism, but, as the present study suggests, a general attitude to war as such, which tries to rationalize it away.

SYSTEMS OF DETERRENCE

Kahn's basic concept, condensed to its most simple expression—too simple, really, in view of the fantastic complexity of the problems—is that it is not admissible to cling to the traditional view held by nuclear scientist and public alike, that thermonuclear war will never be fought because of its horrors, and that when it is fought it will simply mean the end of humanity, indeed doomsday.

The balance of deterrence may be made as stable

[8] *Thinking About the Unthinkable,* pp. 18 f.

as humanly and technologically possible; its stability can never be considered absolute. Central war may break out through miscalculation, error, human failure, or overwhelming political force. Careful estimates based on mathematical and statistical studies by the Stanford Research Institute and The RAND Corporation seemed to prove that a thermonuclear war, at the present moment, in spite of the horrible loss of human life and destruction of values which it would cause, might not altogether exclude the reconstruction of a civilized society in the nations afflicted. In one of the seventy tables (Number 3, p. 20) which, in Herman Kahn's book *On Thermonuclear War*, depict the consequences of nuclear war for civilization, life, economy and culture, we find the following estimate:

DEAD	ECONOMIC RECUPERATION
2,000,000	1 year
5,000,000	2 years
10,000,000	5 years
20,000.000	10 years
40,000,000	20 years
80,000,000	50 years
160,000,000	100 years

The figures refer to the United States and are based on the assumption of a population of 180 million at the time of the outbreak of the war.

An intelligent strategy must be planned, and can be planned, first, to avoid holocaust, and second, to reduce the losses if deterrence fails. Such measures are possible, but only when we accept the challenge, discard the taboo hanging over all thinking concerning this kind of catastrophe, and devise rational attitudes and countermeasures. From this Kahn deduces a series of proposals for official planners and private thinkers. They are: we need better planning and analysis; we must avoid placing over-reliance on strategic deterrence; we must be willing to allocate necessary resources to defense; we must take seriously the fact that we have an enemy, the Soviet Union; we must take seriously the fact that it is our problem to endure safely into the middle of the next decade.

Kahn then carefully analyzes American military policy in the light of its objectives. These were in 1962 —and we may add they will remain in 1972—deterrence of three types: limitation of damage in case of war; improvement of stability; and introduction of measures of arms control. He describes these objectives as follows:

1. Type I Deterrence is designed to discourage a large nuclear attack on the military forces or population of the United States by threatening the attacker with a high level of retaliatory damage.

2. Type II Deterrence is designed to discourage extreme provocation or aggression, short of a large direct attack on the United States, by the threat of nuclear retaliation against the Soviet Union. An example of such provocation would be a nuclear or all-out conventional strike against Western Europe.

3. Measures to improve the war outcome aim to make the nation able to fight, survive and terminate the war. The essential requirements are forces that can endure over a long period of time, civil defense, and a command and control system able to change war plans and to bargain with the enemy.

4. Measures to increase stability aim to exclude the possibility of thermonuclear war by error or accident.

5. Comprehensive arms control attempts to stop or limit the arms race and the use of force for settling international disputes.

6. Finally, type III Deterrence, listed at the end since it is not concerned with thermonuclear war, is designed to deter aggression on a lower level than those covered by Deterrence II. It proceeds by means of the peaceful achievement of political objectives, or of such not so peaceful tactics as limited war, controlled reprisals and intervention against subversion.

SIGNALS TO THE SOVIET UNION

Both the lectures and the book by Herman Kahn, with their sober listing of megatons, of millions of dead, and evaluations of the effects of civil defense measures and of threats, had a double effect. On the one hand, they horrified many people as a medical treatise may horrify the unprepared layman. On the other hand, they opened the way to a rational look at the problem of deterrence by military planners in the United States—and probably in the Soviet Union as well.

Such, indeed, was the intention. It was hoped that an objective assessment of the possible effects of weapons in the hands of both super-powers would prepare a common ground for understanding common problems. Kahn intended to stress how universal was the interest in the stability of deterrence. The analysis of the facts created by the existence of thermonuclear weapons systems would, it was hoped, be understood by the other side.

The importance of this particular effect of the new American studies on problems of deterrence, whoever their authors might be, cannot be overestimated. Since avoidance of war by deterrence is based on the enemy's best possible understanding of the risks a certain course of action would incur, it seems essential

113

that a common language be used. This language may employ words. It may equally well employ signals. Such signals include the development of new weapons systems and the dissemination of the relevant information; nuclear tests, or cessation of tests; measures of civil defense; deployment of strategic forces; the orbiting of satellites; moon shots; the raising or lowering of military budgets; proposals for arms control. That an exchange of signals is going on is evident to every discerning observer. We need only mention, as examples, the shooting down of a U-2 in 1960 over Sverdlowsk, the meeting of President Kennedy and Chairman Khrushchev at Vienna in 1961, the building of the Berlin wall the same year, the Cuba crisis in 1962, the test ban agreement in 1963, the McNamara defense budget in 1964.

It also seems likely that the exchange of strategic ideas encouraged from the American side has begun. The book, *Military Strategy*, edited by Marshal V. D. Sokolovskii, was published in the Soviet Union in mid-1962. By 1963 two translations with interpretative introductions had appeared in the United States.[9] In November of 1963 a new edition with minor changes was published in the Soviet Union. Most of the alterations were made for internal reasons, but some seemed to reflect comments that had been made in the American editions. The second edition and the commentaries in the Soviet press implied that the West was to understand that Moscow's strategic posture had gained in flexibility, and that, for example, escalation

[9] *Soviet Military Strategy*, translated and with an analytical introduction annotations and supplementary material, by Herbert S. Dinerstein, Léon Gouré, Thomas W. Wolfe. A RAND Corporation Research Study (Englewood, N.J., 1963); *Military Strategy, Soviet Doctrine and Concepts*. With an introduction by Raymond L. Garthoff (New York, 1963).

of an armed conflict into major nuclear war was no longer thought inevitable.

The arguments of American strategic analysis that hold limited war possible are no longer rejected, although much scepticism remains. And Soviet theory has added to the body of existing doctrine a useful distinction between "local" war and "limited" war. A local war is limited in the geographical sense, but may be fought with every kind of weapon. Limited war, on the other hand, is, according to this definition, limited both in its geographical extent and in the weapons used.

In his speech on April 20, 1964, Chairman Khrushchev, announcing unilateral but reciprocal steps in reducing the production of plutonium and weapons uranium, spoke in terms consonant with those used in American theory. He referred to the "nuclear rocket shield, reliably safeguarding the security of all countries of the Socialist community."[10] Without the conspicuous role of strategic writing in the United States, this means of communication would, obviously, never have been opened.

It is important to note, at this point, that the scientific discussion of politico-military problems in the United States up to 1965 was oriented exclusively toward the strategic balance between the United States and the Soviet Union, and toward deterrence of the rulers in Moscow. Although for the policy-makers in Washington, deterrence of Communist China and of Cuba was an ever-present problem, it was relatively unimportant, so that strategic analysts never seemed to take it seriously.

We find the pragmatic touch even in thinkers whose

[10] *The New York Times,* April 21, 1964.

methods favor the use of abstraction. The object for them is and remains the relationship to the Soviet Union; the eye remains fixed exclusively on Soviet power, since this is the only power complex from which experience can be derived. This explains why studies of relationships with allies have been neglected. The effects of this neglect are now fully visible. Whereas answers to the major problems existing in the East-West conflict may be found in the literature on strategy, little guidance is provided for the handling of problems like the emergence of independent nuclear power in allied countries, the access to nuclear power within an alliance, and the strategic role of neutrals in peace, war, or negotiations about arms control.

If a new world power emerges, or if a war breaks out other than the dreaded conflict between the United States and a Communist power, the books will have to be rewritten. These problems, among others, will be the subjects of coming studies, and have in fact already been put on the loom in one or another research institution.

PROPOSALS FOR LIMITED STRATEGIC WAR

The possibility of communication between the Soviet Union and the United States may be a by-product of strategic theory. Not a by-product, but of central importance, is the power of the theories to dispel the image of unavoidable thermonuclear exchange once a conflict crosses the lowest imaginable threshold. In thus establishing communications, the powers may have avoided catastrophe and may actually help us to reach the middle of the next decade. War games which develop methods by which escalation of limited

war may be avoided do not necessarily prove that it
will be avoided. What they do prove is that limitation
is conceivable. Proposals for methods and strategies
that exclude central war are no guarantees against
its occurrence, but they point to solutions that hard-
pressed decision-makers may find useful in moments
of crisis.

There has been a rich growth of proposals of this
kind in the late fifties and early sixties. Most of them
start from the assumption that tensions between the
United States and the Soviet Union can be reduced by
reducing armaments. Yet there are more sophisticated
approaches which try to assess correctly the existence
of weapons systems as elements of stability, and to
develop means commonly described as "collateral"
measures—measures other than reduction of manpower and armaments—designed to make war less
likely if not impossible.

Among the many American writings on this particular subject a book by Oskar Morgenstern, *The Question of National Defense*, merits mention.[11] Morgenstern's intimate connection with the application of the
mathematical theory of games to problems of strategy,
and the early date of his writing (1959), make his
contribution especially significant. His book reviews
in the broadest sense the methods of policy-making
and strategic decision in the United States. His conclusion reflects much credit on the military branch,
which at the time he wrote was already making the
widest use of scientific talent of every kind and drawing heavily on the resources of private and semi-
private institutions, while the civilian authorities, particularly the Department of State, remained very

[11] New York, 1959.

much self-contained. Morgenstern's work culminates in the idea that the very technology that has shaped the menacing weapons systems of our times must be applied to make war impossible.

The old pacifist movement, which was so vocal between the World Wars and was resurrected when the guilt complex developed after the first use of the atomic bomb, brought forward theories promising reduction of tensions and ultimate peace through unilateral steps on the part of the United States. One typical example of this school of thought is Amitai Etzioni's book *The Hard Way to Peace: A New Strategy*.[12] This young professor of sociology at Columbia University proposed a method which he terms "Gradualism," meaning that the United States should proceed by unilateral steps to arms reductions in the hope of inspiring the Soviet Union to take corresponding steps. Gradualism is distinguished from the unilateralism more frequently proposed by these circles in that it makes each unilateral step dependent on an equivalent step taken by the Soviet Union. Etzioni elaborated on the subject in another book, *Winning Without War*,[13] which particularly stressed arms control.

A more balanced approach is recommended in the book *An Alternative to War or Surrender* by Charles E. Osgood.[14] This eminent American psychologist also suggests unilateral initiatives, but he surrounds his proposals with important safeguards. The United States capacity to retaliate in case of attack must not be reduced and such initiatives must not cripple the capacity to meet aggression by conventional weapons with graded conventional responses. The risks ac-

12 New York, 1962.
13 Garden City, 1964.
14 Urbana, Ill., 1962.

118

cepted in undertaking unilateral steps must be graduated according to the reciprocation obtained. Unilateral initiatives will be diversified in kind and place in a sincere attempt to reduce tensions, and coupled with an invitation to the other side to reciprocate. They must be executed at the announced time regardless of whether the opposing side has previously committed itself to undertake corresponding steps, and must be continued over a long period of time. Osgood proposes the setting up of a Strategy Planning Board within the U. S. Arms Control and Disarmament Agency, including thinkers from the Departments of Defense and State, scientists, and representatives of industry, to plan and control the graduated steps in tension reduction.

A related proposal concerns the negotiation of a treaty on No-First Use of Nuclear Weapons. This nexus of ideas has been thoroughly explored since the day when it was first mentioned by scientists in connection with the decision to make the thermonuclear bomb. But as a 1963 publication of the Center of International Studies of Princeton University states, the proposal holds little promise of usefulness and feasibility and is rather proof of the desperate search of American strategic thinkers for new areas to explore.[15]

Another method of using nuclear force to stop aggression without resorting to central war is called by its advocates "controlled retaliation." The theory was developed by, among others, Morton Kaplan at Princeton.[16] This strategy consists of communicating to an aggressor or a would-be aggressor a tangible threat.

[15] Policy Memorandum no. 28 (September 1963).
[16] "The Strategy of Limited Retaliation," Center of International Studies, Princeton University, Policy Memorandum no. 19 (April 1959).

The threat, always accompanied by a message, could be one of conventional or nuclear destruction of an industrial object, a military installation, or even a city, probably after its evacuation had been proposed. Another form of controlled retaliation could be the exploding of a megaton weapon in the vicinity of an enemy target at such an altitude that it might be seen and heard, but would not kill people or destroy anything of value.

We see that such thinking follows very closely the lines of thought of the nuclear physicists in 1945, when, seeking to bar the bomb's actual use against a Japanese city, they advocated a demonstration of it in order to induce Japan to surrender.

All the private theories mentioned here are selected almost at random from countless writings. They have little weight and hardly any influence on official thinking or public opinion. But they may serve to illustrate the preoccupation of a segment of the intellectual world with military strategy which since Hiroshima has become a part of the American dialogue.

The extremely uncertain and at the same time extremely risky nature of such courses of action seems perfectly clear to their proponents, who have themselves called them "bizarre." Other writers—for example, Kissinger—proved easily that "graduated retaliation is either too convincing or not convincing enough."[17] Thus a threat or a demonstration that is too convincing will provoke a pre-emptive strike; one that is not convincing enough cannot save the victim of an attack or otherwise achieve its object.

Surprisingly no writer, analyst or policy-maker has to our knowledge ever admitted or suggested that

[17] *The Necessity for Choice*, p. 67.

graduated retaliation has actually been used to some degree. The reason is evident. National interest and national policy did not allow even an allusion to the fact that some of the nuclear tests conducted by the United States were clearly punitive threats directed at the Soviet Union. The tests were all connected with and used for scientific and technological experimentation in the fields of weaponry and communications. But their timing, perhaps their number and size, and the fact that they were actually undertaken and not postponed or dropped altogether, depended on a strategic decision. The strategic purpose was to retaliate against similar Soviet experiments, breaking the tacit moratorium in the late summer of 1961, and to display force in order to prevent further provocation in Berlin. Thus some of the nuclear test explosions of recent years on both sides may be termed measures of graduated retaliation which, in the long run, proved effective.

FORMS OF STRATEGIC WAR

One of the most important achievements of this period of scientific strategic discussion, in which the Armed Services themselves became more and more active through their own research staffs and through specialized semi-private institutions working under contract, is the creation of a comprehensive picture of all the elements of strategic warfare.

Strategic science distinguishes, according to the most recent writing, between two extremes of strategic retaliatory action: countervalue on the one side, and counterforce at the other extreme of the scale. In between are placed the several combinations of both elements. Countervalue attack, the kind of attack the layman generally visualizes when thinking of central war, and to which many European writers on strategy still cling desperately, is an attack with thermonuclear warheads against cities, with the object of killing as many people as possible and of destroying as many capacities and objects of value as possible. Among these capacities are included the conducting of government operations and the continuation of war preparation and war production. Counterforce attack, on the other hand, is an attack with appropriate weapons of fusion or fission type, or even conventional weapons, strictly against the sources of the enemy's strategic power. In its purest form, counterforce attack is coupled with measures of avoidance; in other words military setbacks, such as the failure to destroy the military target completely, are accepted if such is the only way to avoid the death of a good number of civilians or the destruction of material values other than military weapons.

Between the two extremes further possibilities remain. Herman Kahn lists the following typical cases:[18] counterforce plus countervalue, i.e., destruction of population, of property and of military objects; counterforce plus bonus, for example, destruction of a strategic weapons base, and, as a welcome addition in the course of the action, the killing of people and the destruction of property.

In comparing the relative nature, effect and strength of the several types of strategic retaliation, American theory finds rather surprising, but in their logic irrefutable, results: weapons capable only of destroying cities are not offensive but defensive weapons; weapons capable of destroying the strategic weapons of an enemy are offensive weapons. The reason for the dis-

[18] *Thinking About the Unthinkable*, p. 60.

tinction is easy to grasp. If, let us assume, the United States in a surprise attack destroys the strategic bomber force as well as the intercontinental missile force of the Soviet Union or a sizable part of it, she opens the way for any other kind of attack. She may, henceforward, attack with conventional forces, destroy property and people in the Soviet Union or its satellite and allied countries, or may achieve political aims by mere threats, demands and negotiations accompanied by extreme pressure.

Assuming the Soviet Union were to consider a surprise attack on the United States: if it does not believe that the strategic retaliatory force of the United States can be eliminated at an early stage of the conflict, the Soviet Union is exposing itself to a devastating counterblow. The destruction of American cities and the killing of their population would, therefore, not advance the political aims of the Soviet Union; the attack would be without rational object.

France cannot use its reprisal force for an attack since it is conceived and deployed only for destroying cities. A countervalue blow against the Soviet Union, Britain or the United States by France would certainly provoke, along with a disarming counterforce strike, a retaliatory countervalue strike of devastating effect, which would make the first attack meaningless because nobody in France would be left to exploit it.

The theory is not immediately concerned with the feasibility of a pure counterforce strike and the degree to which it would disarm an enemy and eliminate his potentiality for strategic war. In discussing counterforce as a course of action, theorists assume that an adequate technology exists to warrant a course whose strategic advantages are manifest.

THE ARMS DEBATE

In the presence of an ever-growing complex of strategic thought, of proliferating schools of thinking and of many diverse and more and more sophisticated approaches to the central problems of how to avoid a war and how to win a war, an urgent need arose to create system and order within the exploding science.

Robert A. Levine, an economist on the staff of The RAND Corporation, working at the Harvard University Center for International Affairs under the directorship of Robert Bowie, has produced a full and systematic description of the existing American literature. In his book, *The Arms Debate*,[19] he proposes a classification of the schools of thought and of individual analysts and their opinions according to two main criteria. The first is concerned with the purpose a strategy proposes to achieve, the second with the degree of change at which a proposed strategy aims. The first criterion, purpose, serves to classify aims between those of the pacifists: to make war impossible, or to decrease the probability of war, and more especially of thermonuclear war; and those of the anti-Communists: to stem the advance of Communism, to prevent it or even to liberate the captive nations. There is a wide range of varying purposes in between. The second criterion, degree, is concerned with the variety of positions between the approach generally encountered throughout American history in the persons making decisions of high responsibility—described as the marginalists—who try to balance competing considerations, and that of the representatives of systemism, advocates of unconditional systematic change.

[19] Cambridge, Mass., 1963.

Levine thus establishes a spectrum of schools, which he describes in the following terms:

> Systemic anti-war,
> Marginal anti-war,
> Marginal middle,
> Marginal anti-Communist,
> Systemic anti-Communist.

Under systemic anti-war we would place writers like Bertrand Russell. Under marginal anti-war we may place George Kennan, Walter Lippmann, Amitai Etzioni, and Charles Osgood. Under marginal middle we find practically all the writers mentioned in this study as being representative of American strategic thought, like Dean Acheson, Bernard Brodie, Thomas Schelling, Henry Kissinger, Herman Kahn, William Kaufmann, Albert Wohlstetter, Arnold Wolfers, and many others. Under the marginal anti-Communists fall Robert Strausz-Hupé, Stefan Possony, William Kintner. The systemic anti-Communists finally, are represented by men like Senator Barry Goldwater, Alexander de Seversky, and General Thomas S. Power.

The systemists represent, on the one hand, the position of a wide segment of the "liberal" intellectuals and, on the other, deep-rooted convictions of the inarticulate masses. While the marginalists on both the anti-Communist and the anti-war sides represent interesting views but do not exercise notable influence, the middle-marginalists have been influential in shaping the private and official strategic thought that may later be translated into decisions.

How strong is their real influence? This is a question frequently asked in American circles concerned with strategic thinking. A dispassionate observer is inclined to conclude that they have been instrumental in shaping policy to a much higher degree than the American public realizes. The debate among this group turns, as we have seen, about issues such as combinations of strategic deterrence and capacity for limited war and sub-limited war, arms control, collateral measures, unilateral approaches, political approaches and war termination. They are immediately concerned with questions like: How effective is strategic counterforce? How credible is a first-strike capacity? What is the effect of civil defense on the strategic balance? What is the best way to control Western nuclear deterrence of Soviet threats to Europe? How heavily should the defense of Europe depend on battlefield nuclear weapons? How can war be terminated if deterrence fails?

The systematic survey of the whole field shows a surprising wealth and completeness of American research, of scientific exploration and constructive, imaginative thinking. It may be termed surprising since up to the end of World War II the American scene was characterized by the scarcity of strategic study. The reasons for this we have explored, and we have indicated the motivations behind the recent development.

American strategic thought has by now overcome the reluctance to admit power as an element of national policy. The strict separation and division between policy and power has been broken down. Strategy appears in its true, complete sense so aptly expressed by General Albert C. Wedemeyer: "Grand Strategy is the art and science of employing all of a nation's resources to accomplish objectives defined by national policy."[20]

Yet we find remnants of basic patterns of thinking throughout the arms debate. We may mention, by way

[20] *Wedemeyer Reports!* (New York, 1958), p. 81.

of example, the prevailing empiricism that tries to develop theory out of known fact, to wait until "all facts are in" before proceeding on a further step. We may mention bipolarism in strategy, the exclusive preoccupation with the one and only problem of opposing Soviet power. We may again refer here to the moralizing aspects, which tacitly assume that the United States of America is always right, and that the deployment and use of force is always equivalent to the punishment of a wrongdoer.

National defense even now is not deeply felt as a permanent need of the republic, but rather as an answer to an existing, easily defined and recognized threat. One can observe that no sooner does the tension between East and West seem to be easing than there ensues a considerable relaxation of the defense effort of the United States. One can already hear the argument that NATO—since it was conceived as a response to a clearly defined threat—might now be reconsidered. These aspects, however, are not surprising, since we know that for more than a century they dominated all thought devoted to matters military. And they are far outweighed by the enormous advances made in both theory and practice since the conclusion of World War II.

VII

Advanced Thought Applied

TECHNOLOGY AND STRATEGY

We have now before us the question as to what extent strategic thought and theory as developed since the end of World War II shape the national strategy of the United States of America. In this context another problem unfolds: How have strategic theory, technology and planning in the military field achieved the interpenetration that now exists?

Since the beginning of 1961 strategic doctrine has gained distinctive outlines and improved stability. This is due on the one hand to research, which has advanced to a point where the existing problems and those most likely to develop in the future can be clearly visualized, analyzed, and understood, and the best solutions proposed. On the other hand, the evolution of technology greatly contributes to stability. It has reached a point where a wide range of technological possibilities are available from which to choose.

A great technological breakthrough capable of modifying the technological environment seems most unlikely in the immediate future. No invention on the order of importance of light thermonuclear devices, of rockets by which a payload can be orbited around the globe, of solid propellant missiles, or of the atomic submarine is expected in the near future. This can be said, however, only with the reservation that all tech-

128

nological breakthroughs of the recent past seemed unlikely before they occurred. Missile defense, the applications of lasers and masers and similar techniques all still seem to be very much in the experimental stage. Biological, radiological and chemical warfare, in spite of the broad scientific development in view, do not seem to be real military probabilities now.

Whereas in earlier stages technological invention out of which new weapons systems could be devised was the basic factor on which strategy was built, the roles are now reversed. The wide range of possibilities and capabilities existing today enables the planner on the highest level to ask first, "What do I want to achieve?" With this leading question answered, he begins to design the strategy appropriate to his goal, and then chooses the tools, the weapons systems and their deployment suitable for implementing the strategy agreed upon. This is new indeed.

Such an attitude was unthinkable as long as the military planner, the policy planner and the scientist each operated on a different level, without sufficient knowledge of each other's work. We have seen how the outlook has changed. A new concept of national interest grew out of the involvement in World War II, out of policies like the Truman Doctrine, the Marshall Plan, and the North Atlantic Treaty. A new generation emerged from the war, for whom economics, diplomacy, sociology, nuclear physics, military strategy, power politics, systems analysis, and psychology seemed familiar subjects that could be related to the ever-present East-West conflict.

Historically, the initiative for new approaches has come from the Armed Services rather than from the civilian branch of government, the agency responsible for shaping national policy toward allies and opponents. As the necessity arose for the Air Force, the Navy, and the Army—in that order—to develop new generations of weapons systems and to evolve their war plans, they were required to formulate clear views of needs and feasibilities. Since their budgets included large amounts for research, they could invite non-profit institutions to work for them under contract, and to select and pay for the necessary outside talent. As an early example of this kind of research we might mention an extensive study by The RAND Corporation for the Air Force on selection and use of strategic air bases.[1] The volume, completed in April 1954, was originally a classified document, not released until 1962.

SEMI-PRIVATE INSTITUTIONS

As an (unclassified) example of how strategic problems are submitted to private research organizations, we can cite a list of recent contracts awarded by the U. S. Arms Control and Disarmament Agency: techniques of monitoring production of strategic delivery vehicles, to Bendix Systems Division; progressive zonal disarmament, to Raytheon Company; statistical techniques for use in inspection of arms control measures, to Mathematica, Princeton; problems related to inspection systems, to the Institute for Defense Analyses.

One should note here that the Armed Services could not have made such effective use of civilian talent had they not themselves engaged in scientific research, utilizing the help of service personnel able to describe the problems, to ask the pertinent questions, and to evaluate the answers. It was most significant that Sec-

[1] A. J. Wohlstetter, F. S. Hoffman, R. J. Lutz and H. S. Rowen, *Selection and Use of Strategic Air Bases*, R-266 (Santa Monica, Calif., 1963).

retary of Defense Robert McNamara nominated an economist from RAND, Charles J. Hitch, to the post of comptroller with the position of Assistant Secretary of Defense.

Along with its own scientific staff the Navy employs groups at the Office of Naval Research and the Operations Evaluation Group at MIT, the Department of Defense's Office of Defense Research and Engineering, the Ballistic Missile Defense Advanced Research Projects Agency, and the Institute for Defense Analyses (IDA). There are, in all, about three hundred and fifty non-profit organizations, three hundred research centers at universities, and more than a thousand research organizations of industrial companies and private foundations engaged in solving problems more or less related to military security and strategy.

The problem of any possible conflict existing between the "inventor" or innovator, especially when he is not part of the military establishment, and the professional military technician, planner and strategist, has practically vanished, at least as far as the United States is concerned. In Britain, the Navy asserts that throughout the World War it took seriously the ideas of outside technicians and strategists and always gave them an objective hearing. This circumstance may have had something to do with the personality of the Prime Minister, who so often complains in his historical writings about the closedness and conservativism of the Armed Services. In most other countries, we assume, the military still cling to their exclusive prerogative of knowing what is good for the national defense.

In the United States, the development of new weapons systems, the evaluation of strategic systems, and research in general are, in the majority of cases, done at the specific invitation of the Department of Defense or the Armed Services singly. These invitations are generally in the form of development or research contracts. But private industry and private research institutes may equally well offer their new ideas, and they do. If such ideas are approved, then the Department of Defense may support and finance the ensuing research and development.

Private writing on strategic subjects will of course not easily reach and influence the strategic decision-makers. But it readily reaches the advisers and specialists on the several levels of the military hierarchy, since they generally belong to the same generation and the same intellectual group as the writers in universities and institutes. From the advisory level it may gradually penetrate the highest policy-making circles.

There are, of course, noticeable differences in the speed with which particular instances of this occur. Under the Eisenhower administration it took eight years before certain basic concepts were absorbed and translated into action. A good example is the artificial satellite. It was proposed by The RAND Corporation in the late forties, accepted by the Administration as a system worth developing in the mid-fifties, and then practically forgotten until the day of the "Sputnik."

The interpenetration of the military element, the scientific community and industry has grown to an astounding degree. But there are and will always be rivalries and failures of communication. It would be natural that military officers, looking back on a long tradition of isolation from the rest of the nation because of the geographic location of their centers of activity and the professionalism they were obliged to assert against a nation inclined to believe in dilettantism in things military, should have some misgivings concerning too large a penetration of the civilian element into their world. They may regret the fact that they themselves helped to breach the wall between military and non-military affairs. Yet at the same time, they admit that they have generally overemphasized professional specialization. The Armed Services—Navy, Air Force, Army and Marine Corps—in spite of legislation and organizational measures for promoting unity, were slow to overcome interservice barriers. They did not develop a professional military cadre for combined planning and operation, but instead relied on the ad hoc co-operation of specialists from each service. As a military writer and critic of civilian domination in the field of strategic planning and decision says: "This singular failure of the military profession to meet this challenge has provided the lay strategist the occasion to invade the area of military affairs."[2]

But how far strategic thinking in the United States has progressed beyond the point where problems of military professionalism assumed major importance is illustrated by the attention devoted to general problems of strategy in the instruction of the young professional officer in the National Service Academies. At West Point, for example, a course on National Security Problems is taught by the Department of Social Sciences. The course is designed to increase understanding of the domestic and foreign environment in which national security policy is formulated, and "to create awareness of the complex interactions among military policies and between these and other tools of national policy." The reading of the student in these courses

[2] Colonel Robert N. Ginsburgh, "The Challenge to Military Professionalism," *Foreign Affairs*, XLII, 2 (January 1964).

encompasses the whole wide range of modern strategic writing, including expert studies by his own professors—professional military officers. The same holds for the Air Force Academy and the Naval Academy.

The situation of American strategic thinking in the mid-sixties seems to be full of promise. It has permitted the creation of a national defense establishment in the modern sense, directed toward the use of all the nation's resources for the mastery of the infinitely complex problems confronting it.

Quite another problem is the relationship of the military establishment plus science with the political branches of government, and vice versa. Since strategy is the application of all the nation's resources, unless mutual interpenetration of the two complexes is guaranteed, no strategy in the modern sense would be conceivable.

PENTAGON AND DEPARTMENT OF STATE

Diplomacy and foreign policy planning remained, until a very late date—say, 1945—separated by a deep gulf from military planning. Foreign policy planners in the United States were slow to overcome the traditional view that military power is not an element to be dealt with on a day-to-day basis, but rather an auxiliary to which one may have recourse in an emergency —*ultima ratio regis*. During World War II, the military readily sought diplomatic advice, but on a limited basis, to solve specific questions alien to the military mind in a particular theater of war. The diplomats, on the other hand, did not seem to need much military advice. The prevailing attitude is well illustrated by General Eisenhower's decision to leave the terribly important politico-military conference at Casablanca, in 1943, after a few hours, because he was too busy.[3]

Only events after 1946, when Iran required protection against Soviet pressure, 1947, when the Truman Doctrine was developed to protect Greece, Turkey and later Yugoslavia, and 1948, when Czechoslovakia was conquered by Communism, and Berlin blockaded in the same year, brought home the truth that military power had become a permanent corollary of foreign policy. The signing, in April 1949, of the North Atlantic Treaty, the first military alliance of the United States in peacetime, was the symbol of the permanent wedding of policy and power.

When President Truman approved the hydrogen bomb program on January 30, 1950, he requested new over-all assessment of foreign policy and defense policy. The resulting document, prepared within two months and known as NSC 86, was the result of a common effort of the Departments of State and Defense, with a significant contribution from a Council on Foreign Relations scientist, Paul Nitze, later Secretary of the Navy. The document is currently mentioned in politico-military literature, yet is still classified.

The many contributions of non-profit institutions and organizations toward military planning must not cloud the fact that the civilian government departments also sought advice and enlightenment from similar sources. Suffice it to mention here as famous examples the Gaither Report of 1958, which remained classified, the Rockefeller Brothers Fund Report of the same year on the impact of Soviet missile power on United States foreign policy in the widest sense, and the Report *U.S. Foreign Policy, Developments in*

[3] Robert Murphy, *Diplomat Among Warriors* (London, 1964), p. 209.

Military Technology and Their Impact on U.S. Strat-
egy and Foreign Policy, submitted by the Washington
Center of Foreign Policy Research under the leadership of Arnold Wolfers to the Senate Committee on
Foreign Relations in December 1959.

The informal and ad hoc communication between
the Departments of State and Defense, the elabora-
tion of frequent common policy statements, and the
natural and necessary link which existed at the highest level in the person of the President soon proved
inadequate in an environment of threatening war and
subversion. One of the chief instruments for the shaping of institutions that could create a systematic link
between military and political strategy was the
budget. When, after the outbreak of the Korean War
in 1950, the military budget was increased from thirteen billion dollars to forty-two billion, it was a political decision at the highest level, clearly made by those
responsible for the nation's foreign policy. Questions
had now to be answered as to whether the United
States needed more allies, more security agreements,
more deterrence, or all three. The system of foreign
bases required constant review in the light of the question of whether its military usefulness balanced its political cost. Out of this situation there arose the practice for the Department of Defense to communicate
with the Department of State over its own budget proposals. Money requirements created a very strong link.

While frequent exchanges had always taken place
between the Departments of State and Defense on
the higher levels and had been found absolutely essential, they were fully institutionalized only in 1961.
The Office for Politico-Military Affairs was created in
the Department of State and entrusted to a Deputy

Assistant Secretary. This office maintains close contacts with its opposite office in the Department of Defense, and encourages a permanent exchange of information and thought at all levels. It delegates foreign service officers for long periods of study and indoctrination at the Armed Service Colleges and accepts in the Foreign Service Institute officers of the Armed Services. It provides advisers to the Service Academies. A personnel exchange scheme gives officers of the Armed Services the possibility of working for long periods in the Department of State, and diplomats the chance to work in the Department of Defense.

In action, this combination of political and military advice and decision-making has been successful in many instances. Never, as far as can be ascertained, has it impaired the primacy of civilian control. On all levels—in decisions on budget allocations, in crisis management, in actual application of power to a given national policy—the highest decision is always civilian. This is guaranteed by the pre-eminent position of the chief executive and the counterbalancing role of the legislature, and is almost never questioned by the military.

KENNEDY, JOHNSON, MC NAMARA

What are then the current strategic doctrines and concepts that have developed out of this threefold penetration of policy, power and learning? The proof of the value of the organization chart and of the imaginative thinking that has been flowing, through so many channels, into national decision-making is in the validity and effectiveness of the prevailing strategic concepts.

137

The over-all strategic policy of the United States has undergone a series of modifications in the course of the years. The modifications were due:

1. to changes in military technology of which cognizance had to be taken;

2. to changes in the strategic behavior of the opposing power and in her military capabilities;

3. to changes in the attitudes and aspirations of allied and uncommitted nations, modifying the political environment;

4. to changes in strategic theory, brought about by deeper scientific insight into the nature of modern war, particularly nuclear war.

These resulting modifications have been widely misunderstood, especially in European military and political circles. Conventionally trained and ill-informed writers and speakers attributed them to a natural inconsistency prevailing in the United States and to willful mishandling of such important issues as alliances. Nothing could be more erroneous.

During the Kennedy administration, American strategic thinking and policy were gradually brought into a better defined form. We cannot call it final, since nothing is final in the changing world of power; yet it has been set on enduring foundations. Strategic analysis will continue and reveal new aspects of the manifold problems. The arms debate goes on inside the United States and, with ever-increasing vitality, in the whole world. But concepts, a terminology and methods have been developed, which now give the debate a clear outline.

The new strategic doctrine was enunciated in the Special Message on the Defense Budget submitted by President John F. Kennedy to Congress on March

28, 1961.[4] The message clearly outlines the new relationship of policy and power. It states that the Secretary of State has been consulted by the Secretary of Defense on this reappraisal of strategy. "Diplomacy and defense are no longer distinct alternatives, one to be used when the other side fails—but must complement each other." In eight points the main principles of American strategic thought as applied by the Administration are then put forward.

Deterrence of war, general or limited, nuclear or conventional, large or small is the primary objective of strategy. A second and equally important objective, always connected with the primary aim, is the provision of support for the diplomatic settlement of disputes and bargaining power for achieving some degree of arms control.

Strategic arms and defenses must be adequate to deter any deliberate nuclear attack on the United States and its allies, and, since the United States renounces the idea of a first strike, must be able to survive a first strike and to retaliate powerfully, even under prolonged re-attack.

The United States forces, in combination with those of the allies, must be strong enough to deter non-nuclear, sub-limited and guerilla warfare in cases that do not justify general nuclear attack. If a major aggression cannot be repelled by conventional forces, the United States must be prepared to take whatever action is appropriate. All responses must be suitable, selective, swift and effective. The danger of irrational or unpremeditated general war must be eliminated; the principal instruments here are communications,

[4] *Congressional Quarterly Almanac,* 87th Congress, 1st session, XVII (Washington, D.C., 1961), pp. 899 ff.

prevention of surprise attack, an end to the arms race, and prevention of the spread of nuclear weapons.

All arms must be subject to ultimate civilian control and command at all times, in war as well as in peace. All participation in a conflict, use of nuclear weapons, and escalation from small war to a large one must ultimately be decided by the highest civilian authority.

The next representative and comprehensive statement of strategic policy was made by Secretary of Defense Robert McNamara on June 16, 1962, at the University of Michigan.[5] It introduced an important new aspect, prepared by strategic theory, but not previously mentioned by President Kennedy—counterforce strategy.

Corresponding pronouncements were made later both by President Kennedy and by President Lyndon B. Johnson. Secretary McNamara explained the strategic concept again on January 27, 1964, before the House Armed Services Committee in a statement on the defense program for 1965/69, and President Johnson confirmed it in his special message to Congress on January 18, 1965.

It is difficult, therefore, to see how misunderstandings about the principles of American strategy are still conceivable.

DETERRENCE I TO III

Over-all strategic nuclear power has been built up to a level where it can safely maintain the strategic balance. It has been made invulnerable to a high degree. The strategic bomber force is maintained at an elevated level of alert, and its systems of communica-

[5] *Department of State Bulletin*, XLVII (July 9, 1962), 64–69.

tions and command have been made safe against surprise attack. The missile force is deployed on hardened sites within the United States. The number of missiles has been and is still being greatly increased by the addition of the solid fuel "Minuteman," which can be kept in constant readiness. The system is supplemented by the Navy's missile force, consisting of nuclear-propelled submarines armed with "Polaris" missiles.

This nuclear force is designed to deter aggression both nuclear and conventional. It is designed, moreover, should deterrence fail, to win the war and make the survival of organized society possible. To this effect, it is so targeted that in case of a surprise attack against the United States or an allied nation, or a nuclear attack growing out of limited engagements, the enemy's military power will be destroyed by a massive counterblow. This blow aims at the destruction of all the Soviet Union's strategic forces, both the portion that can reach the United States and the portion of Soviet striking power able to reach only western Europe or other neighboring countries and seas. For the execution of this mission, both strategic missiles and bomber forces deployed in the United States and those stationed in Europe and on the surrounding seas would be employed.

In addition to this capability for an all-out counterforce strike, enough invulnerable thermonuclear striking power is deployed to destroy the enemy's cities and society if he drives the United States to do so.

This combination is considered to be the strongest possible deterrence against major attack against the United States or an ally or both, and at the same time the strongest incentive to refrain from striking against cities and the population (Deterrence I and II).

141

The strategic decision underlying this system of deterrence is based on a complex system of values. First in importance is the wish to be able to survive nuclear war and to terminate a war. This is naturally desired, in the first place, for the country itself, its people and the allies, then for the neutral and uncommitted countries, but it extends as well to the enemy, whose total destruction is not contemplated.

"Victory" has assumed quite a different aspect from the idea of victory in earlier American thinking, when it was visualized as complete destruction of an enemy's capabilities to resist the will of the conqueror, according to the pattern of the wars against the American Indians, against the Confederacy, against Germany, against Japan. Humanitarian and moral considerations, and just war theory have further influenced the determination to begin by dealing a counterforce blow, even in case of utmost provocation.

Finally, a strategic consideration in the narrower, military sense is important. A disarming strike, eliminating the enemy's strategic capabilities, would open the way either to conventional conquest of the enemy territory, or to any other method of war termination and achievement of the political aims of the war.

Deterrence III is designed to prevent limited war, both conventional and nuclear. The strategy evolved for putting into effect this type of deterrence depends upon a wide field of weapons systems, ranging from medium-yield and medium-range nuclear weapons down to conventional weapons, air transport capabilities, police forces, mobilizations, maneuvers, and diplomatic moves. All these means are available today, and their use has been rehearsed.

A strategy professing to deal with every kind of threat with appropriate means and on the levels corresponding to the nature of each—a strategy of "flexible response"—has to be able to draw as well upon an arsenal of highly diversified sub-military measures. If Deterrence III fails on any of its many possible levels, the actual application of the strategies so designed will come into play. Application will be strictly geared to the kind and degree of active threat or actual attack. Beginning February 1965, the war in Vietnam became a striking example of systematic employment of these principles.

Countermeasures may begin with defensive moves with only conventional weapons, but not necessarily so. Small nuclear weapons may be used from the very outset by the theater or even local commander as soon as the corresponding authorization from the Supreme Command has been given. Such an authorization is likely to be of a general kind. The use of nuclear weapons would be limited, restrained and restricted, by the commander himself to the actual needs of the battle. But there must be no doubt in the mind of anybody that nuclear arms might be used as soon as American troops, in areas where American ground, air and naval units are operating or participating in any way in the defense, were seriously attacked. It was suggested that there is no government which could face public opinion if it let the American soldier fight a serious battle against a serious foe without permitting him to use his best and most powerful weapons. If nuclear weapons were not used in the Korean crises of the winter 1950/51 it was because the nuclear arm was then still in its infancy, and because the Korean War was a war of coalition, in which the voices of the allies counted as much as public opinion in the United States. The experience of the Vietnam War, however, seems to indicate an extreme reluctance to escalate to

143

the level even of limited employment of the smallest atomic weapons; a reluctance much more marked than current strategic theory had expected.

That use of nuclear weapons on the battlefield could lead to escalation into general nuclear war is generally accepted as a possibility and an inherent risk of any confrontation. But it is a risk for the enemy as well, which he has fully to take into account. The threat of —not with—escalation is one of the most powerful weapons of deterrence. It is strengthened by the very nature of escalation, which escapes calculation and is difficult to predict. American strategy is, therefore, based on the gradual use of a whole wide range of available weapons which escapes calculation by the enemy. It always holds out to an enemy the possibility of stopping the escalation on a low level, if he is interested in limiting the war. This use of the possibility of escalation as a weapon naturally excludes any pre-arranged and previously announced scenario of limited war, such as the introduction of a "pause" of so and so many days after such and such defense measures, as imaginative writers have sometimes proposed.

Deterrence of sub-limited war (subversion, infiltration, revolutionary movements), which might be termed Deterrence IV, is a field that is not yet fully explored and may never be, since it presents an infinite variety of possibilities. Accordingly, no definite strategy has been evolved, and the United States defense establishment has only recently begun to set aside troops and weapons for this special kind of deterrence and, if it fails, warfare.

An argument once used in the American arms debate, and still widely adhered to by European writers, turns upon the question whether conventional capabilities do not perhaps reduce the credibility of nuclear deterrence. This has been asserted very strongly. The theory of opponents of conventional forces holds that the existence of such forces may encourage an aggressor, since it expresses the intention of the defender to use such forces and not to turn to nuclear weapons, so that the risk of escalation seems less.

This erroneous argument has been disposed of by American theory and accepted military doctrine. It is evident, moreover, that Soviet military doctrine also utterly rejects it. The risk of escalation is not reduced by the presence of conventional forces, since even the strongest advocates of conventional forces profess their determination to have recourse to their atomic weapons as soon as those are needed. Deterrence is, on the contrary, strengthened, since a would-be aggressor cannot hope to achieve local success during the time in which an attacked party, having no adequate capability of local resistance, is making up his mind whether to use strategic retaliation, which might be out of proportion with the size and importance of the attack and the attacker's gains.

It is felt in the United States, backed up by responsible theory and fully accepted by the Armed Forces, that the strategy of Deterrence III in limited war has by now been satisfactorily described and can be implemented by existing forces, both American and allied. A strengthening of this important type of deterrence, however, is deemed desirable, and a reduction of forces available for this particular task may be tolerated under no circumstances. Reinforcements of conventional capabilities are required to guarantee a certain margin of security essential to allow for technological change, new tactics and operational methods, defection of allies, and other factors that might influence the balance of power.

145

It is widely admitted that conventional deterrent power is not necessarily to be measured by numbers of divisions alone. Fire power and mobility may outweigh numbers. New operational systems are possible; for example, heavy equipment could be deposited at advanced bases or aboard ships, with corresponding arrangements for an airlift that would, when necessary, bring troops to the equipment from locations where they can conveniently be held in reserve while no crisis exists.

Maintaining the high state of readiness required if the system of deterrence is to be effective naturally poses problems and places the United States under great stresses. The notion of compulsory military service in time of peace is still not fully accepted by the American mind—and probably never will be—since it does not correspond to the American dream of the "peaceful pursuit of happiness." The warlike readiness of the Armed Forces over a long period of time, the end of which is not in sight, can be maintained only by a high quality of military leadership. Readiness is relatively easy to uphold in the Navy, where day-to-day routine requires, even in time of peace, almost the same degree of alertness as war. The same applies to the flying units of the Air Force. The problem is difficult for the crews of the guided missiles, even though an ingenious system in which some missiles are actually fired from an appropriate missile base has been designed to overcome it. For the Army, activity, challenging maneuvers and the excitement of "going places" help to solve the problem.

This whole system of deterrence purports to prevent attack and preserve peace by the very possibility that it may fail. The threat of escalation may help to limit warfare only as long as escalation is possible. Counterforce strategy prevents a strike against cities only as long as it is capable of destroying the enemy's strategic capabilities. Deterrence is effective only as long as the deterring power is prepared to fight the kind of war that would break out if deterrence fails.

ARMS CONTROL

The possibility of failure as prerequisite to the success of a system is, of course, neither reassuring nor satisfactory. This is one of the main reasons why the building of the entire system, both in theory and in fact, has been accompanied by a corresponding effort to stabilize it by methods of arms control.

Notable efforts at disarmament are as old as our century. Generally, they were and still are based on the popular belief that arms engender war, that by doing away with arms we can eliminate conflict and, if conflict occurs, limit its violence and destructive effects. Disarmament proposals have always been encouraged by the considerable propaganda value they carry. Yet proposals for arms control and disarmament have gained new, wider significance since strategic theory has shown their potentialities and their limitations. How important a role is assigned to disarmament is illustrated by the setting up of the U.S. Arms Control and Disarmament Agency in the early months of the Kennedy administration. It is an independent organization directly reporting to the President, conveniently located in the Department of State and in constant touch with both the Departments of State and of Defense.

American thinking on arms control centers today, at least as far as serious official and private exploration of the field is concerned, around improving the stability of the balance of power, and on stabilizing it on a

147

lower and economically less onerous level. The wide variety of solutions recommended, and of results expected, is fully described by Robert A. Levine in *The Arms Debate*.

It may be suspected that the American scholar, now so deeply involved in military matters, felt an urge to square his troubled conscience by giving arms control and disarmament a prominent place in his corresponding studies. A description of the research projects, studies, foundation grants, symposia and government contracts in the field of disarmament and arms control would fill a volume of its own. A collection of significant articles and speeches on this subject, edited by Ernest W. Lefever and published under the direction of Arnold Wolfers, the Director of the Washington Center of Foreign Policy Research in 1962, lists in its selected bibliography not less than 123 publications on the subject.[6]

Among the leading contributions in this particular field are the articles by Thomas C. Schelling, at one time a member of The RAND Corporation, now a professor at Harvard, written between 1956 and 1960. They are reproduced, in essence, in the book, *The Strategy of Conflict*.[7]

Schelling's contribution is a landmark in the evolution of American strategic thought because it shapes three of its essential elements into one whole. Mathematics, games theory, decision theory, operations research, and systems analysis had all contributed significantly to the understanding of the balance of power in the nuclear age. Schelling applies this understand-

[6] *Arms and Arms Control; A Symposium,* Ernest W. Lefever, ed. (New York, 1962), p. 313.
[7] Thomas C. Schelling, *The Strategy of Conflict* (Cambridge, 1960).

ing to the problems of disarmament, destroying on the way the countless misconceptions as to how certain measures of arms control might really affect stability and therefore peace. Although he advocates arms control, one of his central statements is: "It is *not* a foregone conclusion that disarmament, in the literal sense, leads to stability."

The searching examination of the nature and relative value of strategic weapons with a first or second strike capability leads to the conclusion:

> A weapon that can hurt only people, and cannot possibly damage the other side's striking force, is profoundly defensive: It provides its possessor no incentive to strike first. It is the weapon that is designed or deployed to destroy "military" targets—to seek out the enemy's missiles and bombers—that *can* exploit the advantage of striking first and consequently provide a temptation to do so.[8]

The book was followed by a study written in conjunction with Morton Halperin and devoted more particularly to arms control, *Strategy and Arms Control*.[9] The authors take issue with the old concept that arms control opposes the diplomat to the military, and state:

> It is the conservatism of military policy that has caused "arms control" to appear as an alternative, even antithetical, field of action. Perhaps arms control will eventually be viewed as a step in the assimilation of military policy in the over-all national strategy—as a recognition that military postures, being to a large extent a response to the military forces that oppose them, can be subject to mutual accommodation.[10]

[8] Ibid., p. 233.
[9] New York, 1961.
[10] Ibid., p. 143.

In *The Strategy of Conflict* American strategic thought appears at its best. The book reminds us how far European thinking is lagging behind. Only one of the most recent European contributions to this debate —Raymond Aron's *Paix et guerre entre les nations*[11]— may be compared with it. In this context, incidentally, we have to reappraise the generally held image of American and French thinking and writing, since Schelling, the Harvard scholar, seems entirely "Latin" in his brief and elegant presentation of intricate problems, as opposed to the learned, ponderous, almost "Anglo-Saxon" volume of Aron, the French writer.

Whereas many proposals, such as limiting military budgets, prohibition of nuclear test explosions, reduction of military personnel, demilitarized zones and prohibition and destruction of certain kinds of weapons systems, are decidedly of a conventional variety not requiring a great deal of interpretation, the whole new field of the so-called "collaterals" is also highly significant for modern strategic thinking.

An example of a new type of arms control thought is the "open-skies" proposal that President Eisenhower laid before the Summit conference at Geneva in July 1955. As Thomas C. Schelling remarks in his book, *The Strategy of Conflict*, "Surprise-attack schemes, in contrast to other types of disarmament proposals, are based on *deterrence* as the fundamental protection against attack." This assertion is based upon the discovery, described earlier, that the essential offensive weapons are those designed for counterforce purposes. Measures against surprise attack can help to protect the counterforce systems by making them more invulnerable. Thus they reduce the need or the temptation to strike first and, hence, increase stability.

[11] Paris, 1962.

Another type of measure, aerial or other sorts of inspection, works in a similar, indirect way. Inspections may disclose that a potential enemy is preparing for a conventional attack or a counterforce strike, and thus permit the threatened party to issue a warning—if it does not release a pre-emptive strike. The fear of pre-emption may—and this is the real object of inspection—prevent all such preparations. On the other hand, by proving that the opposite side does not plan any offensive move, inspections may equally well remove fear and thereby the danger of an unwarranted pre-emptive strike. And here we find illustrated the fact that in our modern world keeping a military secret may in many cases not be desirable.

Renouncing nuclear tests in the three environments of outer space, atmosphere and water, with the Moscow Treaty of 1963, was significant in a political sense, but to all practical intents little related to the strategy of deterrence and disarmament. The treaty was made when new series of experiments were not immediately needed, and experiments of a wide range, it was felt, could be carried on underground. The agreement is, moreover, so easily terminable in case of overwhelming military necessity that it does not really affect the strategic picture, and, therefore, has not been a real problem for strategic theory.

To put the rapidly developing wealth of research into the service of planning and promoting disarmament, and at the same time to channel it into building a consistent body of theory that can be applied in international negotiations, is the mission of the United States Arms Control and Disarmament Agency. This agency is instrumental in shaping policy with regard to all disarmament negotiations and in drafting corresponding proposals and treaty projects, and has become an example for similar agencies that are being set up, albeit on a much more modest scale, by Foreign Ministries of other nations.

NTH POWER

The deeply explored and carefully constructed edifice of graduated deterrence as a guarantee for maintaining peace, including the whole spectrum of military preparations, arms control measures and political moves, is obviously vulnerable to a rude intrusion from outside. American strategy has, therefore, been reluctant to admit the creation of nuclear forces not connected with its artful construction, since such forces could unbalance its carefully established and secured equilibrium. The proliferation of nuclear weapons—the independent disposition of such weapons systems by power A, B, C to N—has generally been described as undesirable.

This field has not yet been explored as completely as, for example, strategic war and limited war. As the process of dissemination of nuclear technology and nuclear weaponry progresses, it certainly will become an important object of study. And it may well be, nay, it is certain that theory will discover that a stabilizing system of mutual deterrence between the great powers can be so designed, as to withstand the strains and stresses that may be brought to bear on it by the existence of small nuclear forces of nations A to N.

DOCTRINE AND CRISIS

The system of graduated deterrence, of flexible response, in its present form has been applied since 1961. The main fields of application are western Europe and the Mediterranean area, which NATO, in

152

spite of the interior problems of the Alliance, has protected successfully for many years. It is also applied,
with as yet uncertain results, in Southeast Asia. It was
applied, with complete success, in the greatest military confrontation since the Korean War, the second
crisis over Cuba in 1962.

In the crisis that broke out when the Soviet Union
began to base medium-range bombers and ballistic
missiles on Cuban soil, all the elements of flexible response were applied by President Kennedy in a carefully measured and masterful way. Under the shield
of the strategic retaliatory forces, which neutralized
central pressure from the Soviet Union, conventional
forces were deployed around the perimeter of Cuba.
The diplomatic steps demanding removal of the inter-
mediate-range ballistic missiles installed on the island
were accompanied by a partial blockade in order to
prevent a further build-up. The means to attack the
missile sites was held in readiness, while warning to
Soviet personnel was prepared, telling them to assure
their personal safety by leaving the vicinity of the
sites.

In the context of American strategic ideas, it was a
clear case of application of flexible response. The conflict exceeded the stage of diplomatic exchange of
summons and threats and reached the stage of a real
military confrontation, since forces were actually deployed. The United States side had naval units ready
to support a troop landing, the Air Force continuously
flying over Cuba and ready to blast the missile sites
with high explosive or nuclear weapons, and troops
ready to parachute into Cuba and seize the sites. The
Soviets had submarines with torpedoes ready to fire
to sink American transports and naval units, fighters
and fighter-bombers ready to intervene against the

153

Air Force and the fleet, and Soviet ground crews and the Cuban Army ready to defend the bases.

It was the first confrontation of the two great powers in a true military sense. No shots were fired. The governments exchanged admonitions and threats. Although it is likely that, had the Russians not backed down, the United States would have used high explosives only in the bombing of the missile sites on Cuban soil, the danger of escalation was clearly built into the situation.

The Soviet forces in the area were conventionally extremely weak as compared with the overwhelming conventional strength of the United States forces held in readiness. They therefore had no option to fight successfully a limited war about Cuba, nor a local war. Because Moscow was not willing to unleash over-all strategic war over the issue, it entered into the agreement to withdraw the missiles and bombers. The same reason prevented the Soviets from shifting the conflict to another area, such as Turkey or Berlin.

Another case of the application of flexible response, although on a smaller scale than the Cuban issue, was the confrontation in the Gulf of Tonkin in 1964. All the elements developed by strategic theory were present: a previous announcement of the limited character of the reprisals and a limited and adequate retaliation, as President Johnson termed it. An attack by North Vietnamese patrolboats against two United States destroyers was promptly answered by the bombing, with high explosives, of the bases of such boats and of a fuel dump supplying the craft on the North Vietnamese coast. The criticism levelled in the United States against the Administration for having announced the attack before the airplanes had reached their target area gave the government the opportunity to explain in full detail the guiding ideas: to deter a foe by a demonstration of power and determination, and to make clear at the same time that the operation was to be limited and not the opening move of a war. Had this message not been received and understood, the danger of the attack expanding into a conflict with China, and later possibly with the Soviet Union, with the inherent risk of escalation certainly would have existed.

THE MLF

Another application of strategic thought in a highly developed form was the ill-fated Multilateral Force for NATO, the MLF. After having explored several possibilities for limited nuclear sharing within the Alliance, with the object of removing tensions originating in the asymmetry of nuclear participation in the common defense, the American Department of Defense hesitantly produced the project of the MLF. This plan was highly interesting in the context of the development of American strategic thought since it falls exactly into the pattern set up by theory and accepted by the military establishment.

The promoters of the mixed-manned surface fleet armed with "Polaris" missiles were mainly prompted by political motives, such as holding the Alliance together, preventing the dissemination of nuclear weapons, giving the Federal Republic of Germany a share in the nuclear deterrent without actual control of the weapons, unloading part of the financial burden on certain Allies. Since these contradictory political aims defeated each other, the plan was bound to fail. Yet it remains interesting in its military aspects as an example of the application of advanced strategic thought.

The underlying military arguments may be summed up as follows:

1. In the cases of Deterrence I and II, the MLF adds to the reserves that may be used in countervalue countercity strikes, after the counterforce strike or strikes have been administered.

2. The MLF is a valuable improvement of Deterrence II. There are often doubts expressed in allied countries whether the United States would really use its full strategic power to retaliate against a massive provocation other than direct attack upon the American mainland. A strong strategic retaliatory force stationed in or near Europe will, for those who doubt American determination to expose their own population and cities to retaliatory nuclear blows, certainly seems more likely to become engaged, and, therefore, constitutes an increase in the credibility of Deterrence II.

3. The MLF adds significantly to Deterrence III capacity, since it will be deployed in European waters and may be considered a credible threat of a countervalue strike.

4. The MLF is a typical example of a modern weapons system in which strategy precedes technology. The technology was not developed and then applied to some strategy bound up with it; on the contrary a weapons system was designed to fit a political need and to achieve a politico-military aim, in this case the strengthening of the Alliance.

VIII

From Zero to Leadership

THE TIME AND THE INSTRUMENTS

The peace-loving yet military republic visualized by Lieutenant General John Schofield, when he looked back at the end of the nineteenth century over his forty-six years of service in the U. S. Army, was not an environment propitious to military study. It would be wrong to say that there had been no strategic thinking going on in the United States. The writings of Alexander Hamilton (1788), Henry Wager Halleck (1846), Emory Upton (1881), Alfred Thayer Mahan (1890), Theodore Roosevelt (1901), Homer Lea (1909), William Mitchell (1925), Bernard Brodie (1941), and Alexander de Seversky (1942), all mentioned in the present book, are proof that efforts at describing strategic concepts and principles were made by many individual writers. At the same time, non-American strategic literature in a strict sense—as distinguished from historical writing and military manuals of every kind —does not seem very impressive either, except for the great Swiss writer General Antoine Henri Jomini (1779–1869), the eminent German theorist General Carl von Clausewitz (1780–1831), the French military teacher and leader Marshal Ferdinand Foch (1851–1929), the Italian air strategist General Giulio Douhet (1869–1930)—and Mao Tse-tung (b. 1893).

In America, the impact made by existing strategic

writing, with the strange exception of Mahan, never seemed to reach to any depth. Public interest in strategic problems was slight. The military leaders, who had received their professional training at the Service Academies, formed an infinitely small group within a mighty and expansively growing people. They generally met either with indifference to their problems or with the traditional opinion that civilians, by sheer force of patriotism, could easily be turned into soldiers if an emergency arose, and that good civilian leaders would, when war came, make good military leaders as well. Against these tendencies, the military had to guard by defending the military profession and insisting on their status as professionals. This gave them the character of a closed group and encouraged their estrangement from civilian affairs, especially from politics.

The distrust of the military and the rejection of a professional army, which has been the American tendency since 1776, added to their isolation and to the conviction of the military men themselves that they must keep clear of politics. To this were added the fundamental concepts of American foreign policy since Thomas Jefferson: to beware of foreign alliances and, for moral reasons, never to think of using force as a means of furthering national ends. That these concepts were, to say the least, temporarily neglected in cases like Mexico (1847), Spain (1898), Colombia (1903), and naturally in 1917 and 1941, did not affect the image of American policy, and was readily rationalized away by the historian, the schoolteacher, and the political orator.

The empiricism and pragmatism prevailing in American thinking did not encourage the projection of military experience into the future. It decidedly discouraged joint planning on different levels, such as military science, technology, economics, political science, psychology, and natural science, without which, as time has taught, no comprehensive strategy can be developed.

The outcome of World War II changed all that. The scientists penetrated the field of military technology when they proposed the making of the atomic bomb. When the war was over, they hoped to wrest this weapon from the military, to neutralize it, to put it into civilian hands—if possible those of a world government. When this hope failed, they insisted in setting up rules for the use of the new weapons they had conceived. Thus was introduced the arms debate, which still goes on.[1]

The emergence of air power in World War I, and its colossal development in World War II, had depended entirely on the scientist as an adviser, as an inventor. President Wilson had instituted a National Research Council, President Franklin D. Roosevelt the National Defense Research Committee and the Office of Scientific Research and Development. The Armed Services had added scientists to their staffs. In the Second World War, economic warfare, the bomber offensive, had brought the economist and the statistician into closest contact with the military planner and doer. In intelligence work, civilian talent and experience of every kind was needed. For the organization and administration of occupied enemy countries, the military had to rely on the social scientist, political scientist, lawyer, and again the economist.

After the war, the Armed Services and the Depart-

[1] Albert Wohlstetter, "Strategy and the Natural Scientist," *Scientists and National Policy-Making*, Robert Gilpin and Christopher Wright, eds. (New York, 1964), p. 174.

ment of Defense, since they had grown used to the
co-operation of non-military talent and knowledge, included people with university backgrounds in great
numbers permanently within their staffs. Consultants
from universities, foundations and research institutes
were freely used, and, as we have seen, more freely
by the Armed Services than by the political authorities
since funds for paying for their services were more
abundantly available to the military establishment.
The military men had come to like and to respect the
professors, since they were the realists, the masters of
facts, where the conventionally trained officer often
had to base his work on vague opinions.

Industry, confronted with problems presented by
the Armed Services that required fundamental research in science, engineering and systems analysis,
had to resort, ever increasingly, to the universities.
Companies with important defense contracts set up
their own research divisions—notably the airframe industry, and the communications industry. To mention
only one example: Bell Telephone Laboratories, one
of the world's largest private research laboratories, devotes half of its effort to defense problems.

On the other hand, the government has in some
cases entrusted the operation of its own technical facilities to private industrial firms, such as the Atlantic
Missile Range (Cape Kennedy) in 1953 to Pan American World Airways, and the DEW Line to International Telephone and Telegraph. Since the middle of
the fifties, hundreds of thousands of intelligent and
highly trained men and women have been engaged in
defense work. They may belong to the Armed Services, to the Department of Defense, to non-profit organizations set up in close or loose connection with the
Army, Navy, or Air Force, or to university institutes

often working under contract for the government. How different this is from the military community before World War II, which, restrained from within and without, and in isolation, dealt with strategic thought!

The new community produces ideas. It also needs and absorbs ideas. And it is challenged every day by new scientific discoveries, by new technological developments that raise still further an already extremely high level of skill and knowledge. It is challenged by new tasks presented to it by political and military planners and decision-makers, who would not think of tackling an important problem without searching out the most experienced advice.

This development has also its negative aspects. The powers of insight of the natural scientist and the economist have certainly been overrated. From their special knowledge in one specific, admittedly difficult field, popular opinion has concluded that they are omniscient. The military leader has abdicated, too readily, in many cases, before sophisticated discussions of strategic problems by civilian military analysts. Even when we admit that in a modern technological environment all problems of armament, equipment and deployment have to be investigated by scientific methods, the final decision on what is to be achieved, when and how, is one of leadership, and not of science. It would be a grave mistake to believe that strategic theory can replace strategy.

Now that the realm of strategic theory has been well defined, one of the main objects of the arms debate is to find the most profitable and equitable relationship between research and intuition.

EUROPE LAGS BEHIND

Given the closeness of America to Europe and the link established between thirteen European nations and the United States and Canada by the North Atlantic Treaty, which particularly stresses the defense aspects in the common interest, it would be natural that the explosion of strategic thinking in the United States should make its impact on the other side of the Atlantic. Yet the first reaction was one of bewilderment. The men first exposed to American thought were, naturally, European military officers, men trained in the traditionalistic, conservative ways still prevailing.

Curiously enough, conditions under which the military officer had suffered in America for over a century, and to which the European military community seemed then to be immune, are today reproduced to a great extent in Europe. Distrust of the military and lack of interest in military defense, quite natural after a great and devastating war, and negative and superficial anti-war attitudes of political parties and groups among the intelligentsia throw the student of military affairs back into isolation, into professionalization. This situation created the worst possible conditions for the encounter with the new world of New World thought on strategy.

In Europe, scientific strategic study in the modern sense, similar to what we witness in the United States of America, began to emerge only in the mid-fifties. Leading the way was Great Britain with the outstanding military analyst Captain B. H. Liddell Hart and the work done by the Royal Services Institution, followed by the most ambitious and most successful European study group, the Institute for Strategic Studies, founded in London in 1958. The link with America may be easily discerned: its British director had worked as a newspaper correspondent in the United States for several years; the funds were partly provided by the Ford Foundation.

In many other European countries interest in strategic questions developed in due course. It was, however, generally concentrated on questions of arms control and disarmament. This is not surprising. Since the days of the Hague Conferences of 1899 and 1907, the pacifist movements, the students of International Law and the churches had been pioneers in studying the relationship between arms and an international order. It took some time before the problem was understood in a broader, more general context.

Special study groups were set up in the Federal Republic of Germany as early as 1955, in Sweden and Norway in 1960, in France in 1961, the Netherlands in 1962, and Italy in 1964. Some university work in the field of military strategy was undertaken in Switzerland after 1960. Certain newspapers—in France *Le Figaro*, in Germany the *Frankfurter Allgemeine Zeitung*, in Switzerland the *Neue Zürcher Zeitung*, in Great Britain *The Times*—have regularly devoted considerable space to the review of existing strategic thought. Three French writers command our attention. Raymond Aron, in his monumental *Paix et guerre entre les nations*, his *Le grand débat* and many articles in periodicals as well as in his university teaching, offered the most significant European contribution to the arms debate, perhaps the only one transcending the discussion of isolated military problems. General André Beaufre, director of the Institut français d'études stratégiques, founder of the quarterly *Stratégie* in 1964,

163

author of three treatises on nuclear strategy, has begun
to combine European thought with American. Pierre-
M. Gallois in his *Stratégie de l'âge nucléaire* and many
articles has proposed practical solutions for the defense of France rather than considered the results of
objective analysis.

A strong, permanent link with American strategic
thinking, however, has existed only since the Institute
for Strategic Studies in London began in 1959 to or-
ganize its annual assemblies and smaller study conferences.

THE CRISIS OF NATO

All this work did not succeed in making American
strategic theories widely understood in Europe. As
late as 1966, time and again surprise and bewilderment
are expressed about the complexity of American theory. The lack of familiarity with its concepts generally
is rationalized away by alleging inconsistencies in the
theory.

What is true for private and civilian thinkers is even
more true for official circles. The organization which
by definition should link Europe to American strategy,
NATO, has failed in this task. The North Atlantic
Council, even before 1958, which marks the beginning of its sorry transformation from a deliberative
body into a meeting of diplomats reading out communications of their governments to each other, consistently avoided discussing basic strategic questions.

The only facet of American strategic thought ever
completely absorbed in Europe was the doctrine of
massive retaliation, as officially stated from 1952 to
1954. And only in its most extreme form did it seem
to make a lasting impression. In the reactions to the

164

speech by Secretary of State John Foster Dulles on January 12, 1954, only the parts advocating massive retaliation were taken into consideration. The carefully worded passages stressing the importance of local defense were ignored. The many subsequent statements by Dulles and other administration spokesmen, qualifying their earlier attitudes under the impact of experience and developing theory, received much less attention than the original announcement of the "new look."

Europe seemed unwilling to "think about the unthinkable." The initial belief of the scientists, that any war would be central nuclear war, leaving in its wake only ruins and a world in which "the surviving would envy the dead," had struck roots in the European mind. That war in Europe, even without nuclear weapons, would inflict intolerable new devastation was, for very good reasons, a conclusion easily drawn, especially by the German people. Small nuclear weapons, battlefield weapons used in a limited war, made the vision even more disastrous and unacceptable.

The conclusion was, therefore, that war had to be avoided at any cost. For the systemic anti-war school in Europe this meant a renunciation of defense, and unilateral disarmament under the slogan "better red than dead." For the systemic anti-Communist school of thought, it meant a threat with massive retaliation in the most extreme form, even in the case of a minor Communist provocation.

Between these opposed but equally vocal schools of thought, the marginalist schools did not succeed in gaining a wide audience. The middle-marginalist conception, developed in great depth in the United States and accepted as official strategic policy, was, therefore, never really understood and accepted in Europe.

Public opinion and governments simply could not follow a line of thinking that held deterrence as a complete system of threats, consisting of options for responses on all possible levels, to be a much safer tool for the avoidance of war than deterrence of only one kind, such as massive retaliation.

Only one side of the American argument was seized upon: the admission that the threat of massive retaliation lacked credibility, since it involved an exchange of destructive blows between the two super-powers which would produce the loss of life for untold millions of Americans. It was used widely by the anti-war systemists to reinforce their theory that America could not be trusted as an ally. On the other hand, it was and still is used by a school of thought, especially vocal in France, which plans to acquire for Europe or for certain European nations the capability for an independent threat of massive retaliation.

The enormous effort exerted by the United States since 1961 in building up forces for a graduated, and hence credible deterrent is often ignored or misunderstood. It seems only to furnish evidence that the United States Government contemplates the withdrawal of its "shield" and "sword" from Europe. Even the semantic change that put the label "shield" on the strategic deterrent forces, and the label "sword" on the conventional and nuclear forces for local defense, was not accepted. Although it concerned only a popular and convenient symbol, intended to illustrate complex facts of strategy, it was interpreted as a proof of American inconsistency and unreliability.

Describing counterforce strategy in his speech of June 16, 1962, Secretary McNamara stated that the United States had acquired strategic capabilities sufficient to make a significant step toward graduated deterrence. But only one part of the speech was generally found relevant in Europe, and this particular part was interpreted as a sign of lack of determination. Therefore the crisis of NATO, which is certainly the result of historic forces, of diverging real interests, is deepened by the lack of common understanding of the strategic concepts underlying common defense.

AN ATLANTIC COMMUNITY OF THOUGHT

Leading American strategic thinkers are ready to admit that the arms debate and the way it is carried on in the United States have greatly helped to confuse the issues—and the European allies and neutrals. But the American tradition of a completely free exchange of opinions, the full participation in the arms debate of the scientific community, the military and the policy-makers, has made possible the extraordinary and positive achievement of strategic maturity. It has led America from Zero to Leadership. Yet it has at the same time led America away from the rest of the world, which was not ready to follow the daring and imaginative thinking in fields that traditionally had been reserved to the conservative and empirical military mind.

The emergence of schools of strategic thinking in Europe, in Canada, Japan and India, slow and timid as it may have been in many places, proves that it need not always be so. Even from the Soviet Union we receive signals indicating that symmetric terms are used there and similar lines of thought pursued.

It therefore seems more and more necessary—and possible—that the problems of strategy, in the widest sense, should become equally a concern of scholars outside the United States. The destructive power caged in the weapons systems of the nuclear age, delivery systems with a range encircling the globe, communications systems that make the same information instantly available to all nations, have promoted an explosive growth of strategic thought in the United States. Since the same laws of nature apply to the rest of the world, and the same technology shapes more and more the lives of nations, large and small, they will have to participate in an arms debate, the aim of which is to make war unlikely, even impossible, to secure peace in a society of nations in spite of its still being a society of sovereign governments, their relationships still basically governed by power.

The application of scientific thought has helped to control international crises that otherwise might have degenerated into war. Scientific methods of thinking have opened new perspectives for disarmament and arms control. No more the exclusive domain of dreamers and idealists, or a field for cynical exploitation for political propaganda purposes, the limitation of armaments has become a serious concern of responsible governments.

What seems necessary, therefore, is to create an Atlantic Community of thought in the wide field of strategy, including deterrence of war as well as limitation of armaments. This can be achieved. The active participation of American theorists in international gatherings concerned with strategy, the attraction for European scholars of American institutions engaged in strategic research, developed in the last five years, the large degree of financial encouragement given by the great American humanitarian foundations to research organizations outside the United States, have all opened the way to the exchange so greatly needed.

The growth of politico-military thought in the

United States reflects the capacity of the human mind to adjust to new developments and to dominate them. The full participation of other nations who cherish similar traditions and cultivate common beliefs, and who are able to muster the necessary talent, would be the best guarantee for the emergence of an ever-growing community for international security and, finally, peace.

Index

INDEX

Navy, U.S. (cont'd)
passim, 62, 72, 87, 94, 141 (*see also* specific battles, concepts, doctrines, individuals, wars); atomic technology and, 62, 72; deterrence and, 141, 146, 154; evolution in strategy, 130–34, 141, 146, 153–55; flexible response and, 153–55; F. D. Roosevelt and, 50; T. Roosevelt and, 7, 20–21; Wilson and, 3 ff
Nazis, 35–36. *See also* Germany; National Socialism
Necessity for Choice, The (Kissinger), 100, 120 n
Netherlands, the, 38, 163
Neue Zürcher Zeitung, xvi, 163
Neumann, John von, 105; Missile Evaluation Committee under, 82; theories on decision-making, 105–6
Neutrals (uncommitted nations), strategic role of, 116, 138
"New Look" doctrine, 84–86, 89, 165
New Mexico, 58, 68
Newspapers, 163–64. *See also* Publications; specific newspapers
New York, 3, 77, 83
Non-combatants. *See* Civilians: non-combatants
Non-military targets, 67. *See also* Cities; Civilians: non-combatants
Non-profit research institutions, 130, 131, 135–36, 160. *See also* specific organizations
North Africa, 30, 39–42
North Atlantic Treaty Organization. *See* NATO
North Korea, 87–88. *See also* Korean War
North Vietnam, 142, 154. *See also* Indochina
Norway, 62, 163
NSC, 86, 135
Nuclear fission, 61–79, 80 ff, 100 ff, 122. *See also* Atom bombs; Technology
Nuclear fusion, 77–79, 80 ff, 100 ff, 122. *See also* Hydrogen bombs; Thermonuclear technology
Nuclear tests, 114, 121, 151
Nuclear weapons (*see also* Technology; Weapons); control, disarmament (*see* Arms control; Disarmament); and deterrence, massive retaliation (*see* Deterrence; Massive retaliation); and forms of strategic warfare, 121–22; and scientific method and strategy, 105–21 ff, 139 ff; use, non-use, and limited use of, 98–104, 141 ff (*see also* Arms debate)

Obliteration bombings, 54–55, 56, 67, 97
Offensive vs. defensive strategy, 10, 12, 22–37 ff. *See also* Arms control; Defense concept; Deterrence
Office of Scientific Research and Development, 76, 159

One-theater concept, 17–23, 29–30, 37 ff
On Thermonuclear War (Kahn), 106, 109, 110–13
Operations research, 106, 146, 148–49
Osgood, Charles E., 118–19, 125
OVERLORD, 42, 46, 47

Pacific Ocean area, 28–31; fleet, 20–21, 28–31, 37–60 *passim*
Pacifism, pacifists, 16–17, 24, 74, 118, 124–27 (*see also* Arms control; Arms debate; Disarmament); atomic technology and, 69–79, 103; in Europe, 163; scientists, writers as, 69 (*see also* Anti-war school)
Panama Canal, 19, 20–21, 25, 26, 27
Panic, atomic technology and, 70, 71 ff
Paris, 9, 50
Peace movements, organizations. *See* Pacifism, pacifists
Pearl Harbor, 33, 37, 38, 49, 69; as strategic blunder by Japanese, 82–83
Pentagon, policy-planning with the State Department, 134–37 ff
Peripheral warfare, concept of, 41, 88
Pershing, General John J., 9–11, 12; endorses disarmament, 16
Philippine Islands, 19, 29, 37, 38, 51, 52–54; fall of, 38; Lea on Japanese aggression in, 6; as U.S. frontier, 29; U.S. treaties on, 17
Philosophers, 72, 79
Physics and physicists, 62–97 *passim*, 120. *See also* Science and scientists
Planning, 17–37 ff (*see also* specific agencies, doctrines, individuals, wars); for disarmament, 151–52 (*see also* Arms control; Disarmament); interpenetration of strategic theory and technology with, 128 ff, 159–68
"Polaris" missiles, 141, 155–56
Police forces, 112, 142
Policy and power, xv, 24 ff, 157–69 (*see also* Decision-making; Political-military decisions); breakdown of separation between, 126; dissociation of, 26–27, 31–32, 44; new relationship between, 126, 135 ff, 157–69
Political-military decisions (*see also* Decision-making; Policy and power); nuclear technology and, 57–60 (*see also* Technology); post–World War II changes in, 89–104, 105–27, 128–37 ff, 158; schools of thought and, 124–27, 148–49; World War II, 40, 44, 46–48, 55–56, 134–35
Political science, writings from, 95–104 *passim*, 159. *See also* Research institutions

175

INDEX

177

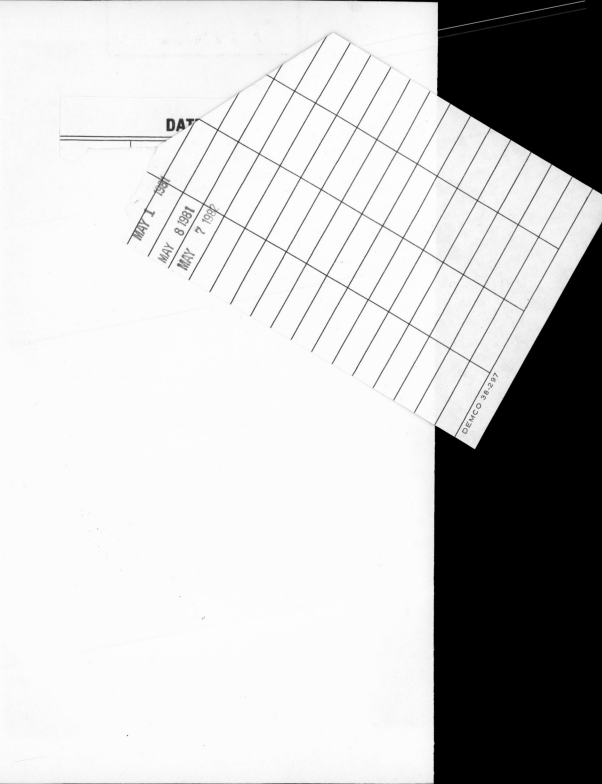

DAT

MAY 1 1981

MAY 8 1981

MAY 7 1982